HEAVENLY REALMS:

A Journey into the Unknown

... ◈ ...

*Discovering the Mysteries of
Heaven and the Afterlife*

John Allen

information contained within this document, including, but not limited to, errors, omissions, or inaccuracies.

TABLE OF CONTENTS

Dedication Page
—Dear Heavenly Father

Dear Heavenly Father,

I come before you with a heart full of gratitude for the opportunity to share the mysteries of heaven through the pages of this book. May your divine guidance and inspiration flow through me as I write, allowing your light to shine brightly in every word and every page. Bless this book with your wisdom and love, so that all who read it may be touched by the beauty and peace of your heavenly kingdom. May it bring comfort, hope, and a deeper understanding of your eternal grace.

In your holy name, Amen.

INTRODUCTION

...◈...

Perhaps the first question that pulls at our hearts is one of our very origins: "Where did we come from?" This question has lingered in the depths of human consciousness since the beginning, inviting exploration through the lenses of science, religion, and philosophy. From a scientific perspective, we trace our lineage through the intricate flow of biological evolution—a story spanning billions of years, from the primordial soup to the varied mosaic of life we inhabit today. Conversely, religious and spiritual narratives offer a different perspective, often depicting our existence as the handiwork of a divine creator, with each tradition crafting its own legend of creation and purpose.

The timeless question "Why are we here?" has intrigued philosophers and seekers throughout time. Why we exist is as varied as the human experience itself, shaped by our beliefs, cultural fabric, and philosophical perspectives. Some find peace in religion or spirituality, while others seek meaning in personal growth, human connections, societal contribution, or the quest for knowledge. Ultimately, the answer to this fundamental question is as varied as human existence itself.

Have you ever wondered what happens after we die? Different cultures, religions, and philosophies have their own beliefs about the afterlife. Some people find comfort in the idea of living forever in places like Heaven, Hell, or through reincarnation, guided by their faith. Others see death as a mysterious unknown, beyond the limits of what we can understand.

Yet, within all of this, one truth always stays the same. The idea of the afterlife is a personal one, based on our individual beliefs, cultural background, and personal stories.

What should you expect to find within these pages? We will touch on many topics, including sincere and meaningful conversations surrounding:

- grief and how our beliefs impact this path
- the concept and belief of Heaven
- the comforting impact of the afterlife
- sharing of near-death experiences
- how scripture plays into our beliefs
- life's purpose and endless possibilities

I invite you to join me on a journey of exploration and introspection. Together, we'll look at the questions of existence and the afterlife, searching for thought-provoking observations we can discuss about Heaven and the afterlife. The destination? It's yours to discover.

CHAPTER 1:

The Unchartered Territory of Grief

I want to personally welcome you to this often uncomfortable and unspoken territory of grief. I would like us to embark together on a poignant exploration of the varied emotions that envelop us after the loss of a loved one. Before we venture further, allow me to share with you a glimpse into my own journey through the ever-shifting landscape of grief. In my previous works, such as *Keep Calm and Cope With Grief*, I introduced you to my heart-wrenching narrative of saying goodbye to my father, sitting beside him as he battled illness, and ultimately holding his hand as he departed from this world. The profound ache of loss was, and still is, numbing. This was compounded by the unfamiliar tasks of arranging funerals, navigating legal matters, and deciphering the enigmatic language of grief.

In my subsequent book, *Life After This*, I went on a quest for understanding, and sought answers in the testimonies of near-death experiences and the subtle signs that whispered of a realm beyond our comprehension.

However, my grief did not stop at that point. With each passing year came new pain—the loss of beloved pets and the departure of additional cherished family members—leaving me adrift in a sea of sorrow.

In the midst of darkness, I found peace in nature, where I could relax. In my next book, *Nature's Reach*, I talked about the soothing effect of the rustling leaves, the gentle touch of the wind, and the quiet company of woodland animals. Despite my grief, I saw the beauty of the natural world and found peace in its unchanging patterns and timeless rhythms.

And now, as I start another book, I invite you to join me in an honest exploration of the changing experience of grief. Whether you are just beginning to face loss, still struggling with the intense pain of absence, or moving through the process of healing, remember that you are not alone.

In this chapter, we will face the unknown and recognize the fear and uncertainty that comes with the departure of a loved one. We will go through the unfamiliar territory of grief, looking for understanding, comfort, and (maybe) even a glimpse of hope together.

So, I ask you: Where are you in your grief? How is your healing journey? Let's try to walk this path for a while, hand in hand, as we visit loss and discuss *what if*'s and *why*'s together.

The Overwhelming Pain of Loss

Many have tried to write on the topic of the unique pain we feel after loss. Lectures and seminars have been held. Books have been written, websites built, and podcasts launched—all in an effort to understand.

So, what is it exactly that we are trying to uncover? Throughout our lifetime, we are met with painful emotions. We can feel betrayed, hurt, panicked, afraid, and angry, just to name a few. Regardless of how these emotions find their way into our lives, they don't tend to stay for a lifetime.

Let me introduce you to grief. This is a complex being of its own. To demonstrate this a bit further, allow me to introduce you to a wonderful, resilient woman.

Erin's Story

Born the middle child, with an older brother and a younger sister, my parents divorced when I was just five years old. Now a woman in my fifties, I have spent the last fifteen years as a therapist, and the last eight specializing in grief. Through educated eyes, I can say, without a doubt, that my parents shouldn't have had children. I am blessed to be here, but they laid a heavy burden on my shoulders—one that required me to break many generational cycles.

From a young age, I faced pain and loss. I was abused, neglected, and left feeling worthless. It would take twenty years of therapy and hard work to alleviate the extremely toxic emotions that came with that baggage. I did the work and created the life I deserved.

Five years back, a phone call altered the course of my life. It pitted me against pain and loss I didn't understand or know how to handle. My baby sister was gone. An animal lover, she swerved her car in the road to avoid a possum; she lost control and, ultimately, her life.

As a grief counselor, those around me leaned on me for support. They all assumed I would be able to handle *their* pain and my *own* with ease. Truth is, I lost the ability to take a full breath the day she died. This was a pain I couldn't describe. I questioned everything in existence. I feared getting into a car and my own life being cut short. Panic attacks and nightmares flooded in like a dam had broken open inside me.

Yet, nobody noticed.

It would take me finding a great therapist to hold my soul through this. What have I discovered? Well, for me, this pain is unlike anything I have ever suffered. I have been physically beaten, assaulted, abused, neglected... yet this was worse. This internal pain, this burn I couldn't soothe, was unrelenting. Time didn't heal me, but it did allow me the space to process. I had to alter my perspective. I know my sister isn't physically here with me, but I take calm and peace in knowing she is all around me. I am soothed believing I will see her again one day. I don't believe our story is over.

My grief is forever. The sooner I accepted that and stopped trying to fight it, the easier I could breathe. It is now a part of who I am, and it doesn't have to be a bad thing. Losing my beautiful sister is now a part of my story, but I focus on how amazing she was when I talk about her. I focus on the great parts, not the tragedy, when her name passes my lips.

***

If you're holding this book, chances are you're carrying a weight heavier than words can express. The pain of loss is a trek through a landscape of emotions so raw, it feels like your heart might never heal. I want you to know that your pain is valid, your tears are sacred, and your healing is uniquely yours.

Losing someone we love is like having a piece of our soul torn away. It leaves a void that seems impossible to fill. The intensity of that pain can be overwhelming, suffocating even. It's like being caught in a storm without shelter, with waves of grief crashing over you relentlessly.

The impact of loss reverberates through every aspect of our lives. It's not just the absence of their physical presence that weighs heavy on our hearts; it's the absence of their laughter, their wisdom, their quirks, and the shared moments that made life feel so full. Suddenly, the world seems dimmer, quieter, and lonelier without them.

Experiencing a range of emotions when a loved one passes away is a normal part of being human. During these times, it's crucial to reach out for support from friends, family, or professionals to assist with grief.

After our loved one has passed away, we often find ourselves grappling with numerous questions and uncertainties about their whereabouts. Personally, my question was: *Where is my dad now?*

My faith assured me that my dad was in Heaven, but I wanted evidence. I felt afraid. *Would I ever reunite with him?* How do we handle loss and grief, with numerous unresolved questions? Does this intensify our grief? If we had confirmation that our loved one was at peace in Heaven, would our grief be significantly less painful? I am convinced it would.

Witnessing Grief

Witnessing grief, particularly when it emanates from someone you hold dear, is an experience that resonates on a profound level and shakes the very core of your existence. To observe someone you love, once a source of strength, shattered by loss is to witness the fragility of the human spirit laid bare.

I recall the sight of my mother, a pillar of resilience in my life, suddenly transformed into a figure of vulnerability in the wake of my father's passing. After 55 years of partnership, his absence left a chasm in her heart: a void that seemed impossible to fill. I stood by her side, watching as she navigated the tumultuous currents of grief, each wave crashing against her with relentless force.

The loss of her lifelong companion cut deeper than mere words could convey. Their love story lasted for many decades, proving the strength of their bond and the deep connection they had with each other. As I bore witness to her pain, I grappled with a sense of helplessness, acutely aware that no words of comfort could assuage the ache in her heart.

In those moments of vulnerability, I witnessed the raw beauty of human emotion—the intricate interplay of love and loss, sorrow and joy. My parents' love transcended the confines of earthly existence, reaching beyond the boundaries of mortality and into the realm of eternity.

If you, too, have experienced the anguish of watching a loved one grieve, you may have felt powerless in the face of their pain, your support seeming inadequate to shield them from the depths of their sorrow. Yet, within that vulnerability lies a profound beauty—a testament to the enduring strength of love that binds us together.

It is in these moments of shared grief that we gain insight into the complex tapestry of human experience, recognizing the interconnectedness of our souls and the depth of our capacity for empathy and compassion. As we stand alongside our loved ones, bearing witness to their pain, we affirm the enduring power of love to eclipse even the darkest of nights.

Grief: The Loneliness Nobody Speaks Of

Carrying the burden of grief can be heavy. We may find it hard to understand and manage. Within this struggle, we may suffer in silence, as if it's a secret we're afraid to reveal.

Grief can isolate us, as if we're alone in a crowded room. We yearn for connection and for someone to reach out and hold our hand in the darkness, but that connection often feels distant.

Now, more than ever, is the time to lean on your people. It may feel like you are alone, but they are there. Reach out your hand, ask for help, and let them support you through this time.

And what about those who have left us? How can we stay connected to them, even as they journey beyond this earthly realm? It's a question that has haunted me ever since I lost my father and watched as others followed in his footsteps.

For me, I choose to believe they never truly leave us. Their presence lingers in the memories we hold dear, in the stories we tell, and in the lessons they taught us. They may not be physically with us, but their spirit lives on in the hearts of the ones who loved them.

So, how can we feel connected to those who have left us? We can do so by keeping their memory alive, honoring the legacy they left behind, and finding solace in the belief that they are watching over us and guiding us from beyond.

But perhaps most importantly, we can feel connected to those who have left us by embracing the love they shared with us in life. Love knows no boundaries, not even death, and it is through love that we can bridge the gap between this world and the next.

Throughout these pages, we will hear stories of connectedness to those who have passed. Unique and thought-provoking ideas that keep us asking the question: *Where do our loved ones go when they die?*

The Weight of Unanswered Questions

As I sit here and write these words, I am keenly aware of the weight that unanswered questions can place upon our hearts, especially in moments of profound loss. It's a path I've traveled many times myself, through the corridors of grief, seeking peace in the face of uncertainty.

The questions that trouble us are familiar, aren't they? *Is our loved one okay? Where did they go? Will I see them again?* These are not just thoughts; they are the echoes of our deepest fears and desires, resonating through the depths of our being. They persistently pull at us, seeking answers that always appear just out of reach.

Within these pages, the goal is to explore the mysteries of Heaven and the afterlife. We will delve into the realms of faith, science, and personal experience, and seek to unravel the enigma of what lies beyond.

I have come across stories that are hard to explain—moments when I've seen a reality that goes beyond what we can understand. I've looked through history, trying to find knowledge in the words of wise people and scholars who have thought about these same mysteries for thousands of years. I've also gone on a very personal voyage, sharing the happy and sad moments of my own experiences, hoping to show the way for others.

But let me be clear: I am not here to offer easy answers or to impose my beliefs upon you. No, my role is simply to serve as a guide—a companion on this voyage of discovery. Within these chapters, you will find details, facts, quotes, stories, and interviews—all laid out before you like pieces of a puzzle waiting to be assembled. Yet, in the end, it is up to you to decide how they fit together.

This journey requires an open heart and a curious mind, embracing what we know and the mystery of what we cannot yet understand. As we start this adventure together, let's do so with courage, humility, and a strong belief in the power of hope.

CHAPTER 2:

Exploring the Concept of Heaven

...◈...

Have you ever looked up at the night sky, thinking about the enormity of the universe, and found yourself wondering about why we can't *see Heaven*? As we look into the unknown world of Heaven, let us first pause to clarify what exactly we mean when we speak of it.

Heaven is a word that carries weighty implications, yet its definition often eludes us; it slips through the fingers of our understanding like grains of sand. Is it a physical place: a celestial abode beyond the reaches of mortal comprehension?

Or perhaps it is a spiritual realm: a sanctuary for the soul to find peace and serenity? Some may even view it as a metaphorical concept—a state of being, rather than a tangible destination.

In our search for clarity, it's important that we all attempt to understand this mysterious term in the same way. The diversity of interpretations allows us to explore and discover new insights and perspectives, which is a beautiful opportunity.

Throughout the ages, poets, philosophers, and theologians have tried to capture the essence of Heaven in words, painting vivid pictures of paradise with strokes of imagination. Yet, no matter how hard we try, Heaven remains a place shrouded in mystery, its true nature hidden behind the veil of mortality.

Let's approach the concept of Heaven with open hearts and minds, ready to embrace all the possibilities it presents. Maybe you perceive it as a celestial kingdom, a spiritual haven, or a symbol of transcendence? Remember that the essence of Heaven lies not in its definition but in the profound sense of peace, hope, and eternal love it offers to weary souls.

So, let's begin this quest for understanding with humility and respect, knowing that in our exploration of Heaven, we may discover not only the mysteries of the afterlife but also the hidden depths of our own humanity.

The Significance of Heaven in Different Cultures and Religions

In every corner of the world, throughout history, humanity has pondered the unknown that lies in the afterlife. From the ancient civilizations of Egypt and Mesopotamia to the modern-day faiths that dot our diverse landscape, the concept of Heaven has been a source of hope for many facing uncertainty.

We'll start by peering into the significance of Heaven in different cultures and religions.

Christianity

The Christian idea of Heaven is all about joy and celebration in the presence of God in a brand new world. This new Heaven has a deep connection to Judaism because of the presence of a city called New Jerusalem, which is thoroughly described in the Book of Revelation. New Jerusalem is surrounded by a wall with 12 gates, each named after one of the tribes of Israel and guarded by an angel. The city is also home to 12 foundations, symbolizing the apostles. Notably, the dimensions of New Jerusalem are specified as a vast square, measuring 1,400 miles on each side, and enclosed by a 200-foot-tall wall. The city is constructed using rare gemstones, some of which are unfamiliar on Earth. A river, known as "the water of life," flows from God's throne, and trees of life line its banks, producing fruit monthly. Those who have faith will bear God's name on their foreheads, and there will be an end to suffering, sorrow, and mortality (Sayler, 2007).

Judaism

Being one of the oldest religions, Judaism could be seen as the origin of our deepest concepts of Heaven. The Jewish scriptures do not clearly mention a Heaven or afterlife, which has sparked a lot of debate on the topic. Two common viewpoints were held by the Pharisees, who believed in an implied afterlife, and the Sadducees, who argued that there was no biblical evidence for it. Jews have developed different beliefs about Heaven over thousands of years. Some of these beliefs involve the righteous dead returning to life after the Messiah arrives. Judaism is more concerned with living life in the present. The idea of Olam Ha-Ba, also known as the "World to Come," implies a future existence where good people are rewarded and bad people are punished, even though the details are not backed by publication (Sayler, 2007).

Islam

Heaven is described as a beautiful paradise reserved for those who have done more good deeds than bad ones, following the teachings in the Quran. It's envisioned as a lush garden where believers relax on comfy couches in a perfectly controlled climate. They'll be surrounded by beautiful, modest women— described as having dark, modest eyes and as pure as the revered ostrich eggs. They'll enjoy drinks from crystal and silver containers while being served by young, eternal companions as lovely as pearls. Believers will be dressed in green silk and adorned with silver jewelry. They'll also get to drink pure, refreshing water from a special source, provided by Allah as a reward for their perseverance and patience (Sayler, 2007).

Hinduism

In Hinduism, there's a concept called Moksha, which is about breaking free from the cycle of life, death, and rebirth. Unlike Western ideas of Heaven, Eastern religions like Hinduism focus more on finding freedom from the illusions and suffering of this world. According to Hindu scriptures like the Upanishads, our actions tie us to this world, which is actually just an illusion. The true reality, called Brahman, is beyond what we can sense. However, because we're ignorant of this reality, we act based on false perceptions, leading us to get stuck in the cycle of rebirth, known as samsara. But if we can overcome our ignorance and realize that we're not separate from Brahman but actually part of it, we can attain Moksha, which is liberation from this cycle of rebirth (Sayler, 2007).

Buddhism

One of Buddha's important teachings is that suffering comes from our desires—coveting things and wanting to be someone. This desire, called tanha, is like a burning fire that traps us in the illusion of our ego. Buddha said this desire keeps us suffering and stuck in the cycle of life and death because it carries on into our next life. What we aim for is Nirvana, which is like putting out that fire of desire and ending suffering (Sayler, 2007).

The idea of Heaven differs among various religions, but it typically denotes a realm or state of being linked to supreme happiness, joy, and spiritual satisfaction. What a beautiful, peaceful thought to aspire to.

Various Interpretations of Heaven

To understand the concept of Heaven, we must look into history, back to ancient civilizations where celestial longing first began.

In the earliest human cultures, Heaven is often mingled with the mysteries of the cosmos and the divine. The ancient Egyptians envisioned an afterlife where the soul journeyed through the Duat, a realm of gods and judgment, guided by rituals and beliefs in the immortality of the soul.

As civilizations started and religions grew, so too did the myriad interpretations of Heaven. In Mesopotamia, the Sumerians believed in a paradise-like land called Dilmun, while the Greeks imagined the Elysian Fields: a realm of bliss reserved for the righteous (Kramer, 1964; Atsma, n.d.). These diverse beliefs reflected the cultural variety of their time, bringing together notions of reward, justice, and transcendence.

Fast forward to the rise of monotheism, and we encounter pivotal figures and events that reshaped our understanding of Heaven. The teachings of Abraham, Moses, and (later) Jesus Christ introduced profound concepts of divine grace, redemption, and eternal life. Christianity, with its promise of salvation and the kingdom of Heaven, offered peace to the weary and hope to the downtrodden.

Throughout history, there have been people with extraordinary insight who have influenced the way people think about Heaven. Visionaries and mystics—such as Dante Alighieri, known for his Divine Comedy, and Emanuel Swedenborg, who claimed to have visited Heaven in his visions—have provided glimpses into the mysterious and indescribable realms beyond, shaping the collective consciousness of humanity (Rowlandson, 2011).

Yet, beyond the confines of religious doctrine, the concept of Heaven has transcended cultural and ideological boundaries, finding expression in art, literature, and philosophy. From the celestial realms of Plato's Symposium to the cosmic visions of William Blake, Heaven has inspired wonder, awe, and contemplation (Via, 2022).

And so, as we reflect on the evolution of Heaven, let us remember that it is not merely a destination but a state of being—a place of boundless love, compassion, and unity. Whether depicted as a golden city, a lush garden, or a celestial sphere, Heaven speaks to the deepest longings of the human soul—a longing for transcendence, for connection, and for eternal peace.

Common Themes and Beliefs Surrounding the Afterlife

As we think about what happens after we die, it's like looking into a huge ocean of beliefs. Each belief is like a wave, offering a different view of the afterlife. People from ancient times to today have various ideas about what happens to the soul after death, creating a colorful pool of beliefs.

At the core of these beliefs is a common idea: the soul. It's the equivocal essence of who we are, moving on beyond our physical bodies. Even though the details differ, the concept of the soul's journey is found in many cultures and religions, giving comfort and hope when dealing with death.

Let's explore together as truth-seekers, not experts. By looking at spirituality, we can extrapolate perceptions about the afterlife.

Reincarnation is the idea of souls coming back to life in different bodies, moving through cycles of learning and growth to enlightenment. This concept is widely accepted across various cultures worldwide, from Eastern mystical teachings to the wisdom of indigenous communities.

Heaven and Hell are concepts found in many religions. They demonstrate the idea of being rewarded or punished by a higher power based on how we live. They make us think about how our actions can lead to good or bad outcomes in the future.

And then, there's the mysterious spirit world, where the boundary between the living and the dead becomes faint, making it possible to connect with ancestors and supernatural beings. This realm is full of secrets but, also, offers the reassuring company of our departed loved ones.

In Hinduism and Buddhism, the soul's journey is represented by Samsara, a cycle of rebirths spanning many lifetimes in search of freedom. This path is influenced by karma, the universal principle where our actions determine our future outcomes, over time (Noonan, 2023).

In mystical teachings, as the soul moves through higher dimensions, it shows the limitless possibilities of human consciousness. This is about awakening and expanding our awareness from the physical world to the endless spiritual realms.

As we think about all these different beliefs and viewpoints, let's remember that we are just travelers on the road of life, looking for meaning and purpose even when things are uncertain. Though we may not know everything, our ability to feel amazed and inspired has no boundaries.

In life, every belief is important for our group understanding. It's always a great idea to welcome different afterlife beliefs because they offer wisdom and compassion.

The Concept of Punishment and Reward

The idea of discovering a forever peaceful place has brought comfort to those in all cultures, spanning many spiritual beliefs. It's like imagining a calm oasis where we can put our feet up and rest, without worries, and enjoy eternal peace.

In this tranquil area where souls rest forever, they are thought to move to a better world after death. This world could be *Heaven* in Christianity, *paradise* in Islam, *spiritual freedom* in Hinduism, or *enlightenment* in Buddhism. It's where souls find comfort, meet loved ones again, and feel happy and wise.

Some people imagine a temporary resting place where souls go through a cleansing process before moving on to higher realms. Whether it's called purgatory, limbo, or bardo, this transitional phase is an important step in the soul's spiritual journey.

Not everyone finds comfort in the idea of an eternal resting place. Some prefer to believe that consciousness ends after death, finding peace in the natural order of the universe instead of an afterlife. This viewpoint is based on atheism or agnosticism, focusing on scientific reasoning for life and death.

Judgement, a common theme in some spiritual beliefs, prompts us to think about what happens to our souls after we die. It's like our actions in life are carefully evaluated on a grand scale, deciding where we will spend eternity.

For Christians, Judgment Day means Jesus Christ comes back. Good people go to Heaven, and bad people go to Hell. In Islam, Qiyamah is the Day of Resurrection. People are judged on their faith and actions, going to Paradise or Hell based on that (Noonan, 2023).

The concept of karmic debt extends over multiple lifetimes, forming a cycle of actions and outcomes that impact our souls across many lives. In Hinduism, Buddhism, and Jainism, karma decides if souls progress toward liberation or rebirth based on their actions and intentions.

As we explore different faiths and viewpoints, let's remember that seeking to understand goes beyond cultural and religious differences. We can choose to take comfort in the idea of an afterlife or welcome the unknown of what happens after death.

Existence and Evidence

In our world, things we can't see are just as important as things we can see. For example, oxygen and gravity are not visible, yet we feel them every day. There are also important things like love, dignity, justice, and hope that we can't see but strongly influence our lives.

Now, think about the idea of a spiritual realm, which is real but cannot be measured scientifically. These are the teachings of the Bible on Heaven. We can't use science to prove Heaven exists like we can locate a place on a map, but that doesn't mean it's not real. Belief in Heaven is based on faith, a strong conviction, rather than a lack of knowledge.

One writer in the Bible describes faith as being unfaltering about what we wish for and implicit about what we cannot vision. "Now faith is confidence in what we hope for and assurance about what we do not see" (*New International Version*

Bible [NIV], 2011/1978, Hebrews 11:1). Christians have faith in Heaven because they trust the Bible, which clearly talks about its existence. However, we sometimes desire something more concrete and easier to prove.

The book of Ecclesiastes in the Old Testament hints that God has planted the idea of eternity in our hearts. "He has planted eternity in the human heart" (*Holy Bible, New Living Translation [NLT]*, 2015/1996, Ecclesiastes 3:11). Since we are created in God's image, we instinctively long for eternal life. This longing for something everlasting is a part of who we are, driving us to seek beyond the temporary things in life.

Though we can't prove or disprove Heaven's existence scientifically, the evidence from scripture and our inner yearnings suggest its plausibility. Christian tradition teaches that God initiated our access to Heaven. Through Jesus Christ, God connected Heaven and Earth by living a perfect life, taking on our punishment, and conquering death through resurrection. This sacrificial act provides redemption to those who believe, offering them eternal life in God's presence (Smethurst, n.d.).

Consider this question: Does God eagerly anticipate our presence in Heaven as much as we yearn for it? This mutual desire shows the strong connection between humanity and the desire for peace in the afterlife, giving us a glimpse of the limitless love and grace waiting for us beyond death.

We will examine biblical references much more in depth within Chapter 5.

Philosophy

It's normal to think about whether such a heavenly place exists. How can we explore this question? How can we bring together philosophical thoughts, personal experiences, and scientific observations?

Let's start by discussing philosophical arguments about Heaven. Brilliant thinkers like Plato and Descartes have explored this concept extensively throughout history. They have looked into places beyond our physical world, using ideas such as Plato's *Forms* and Descartes' mind-body dualism.

Plato, the ancient Greek philosopher, introduced the idea of *Forms*. He suggested that beyond the physical world we see and touch, there exists a realm of perfect and unchanging forms. According to Plato, these *Forms* represent the true essence of reality, while the material world is just a flawed reflection of these ideal forms (Andrade, n.d.). This concept encourages us to think about the possibility of higher realms beyond what we can directly experience, where perfection and truth exist. This idea aligns with the concept of Heaven as a divine place of ultimate truth and beauty.

Moving forward in philosophy, we meet René Descartes, a key figure of the Enlightenment. Descartes explored the connection between the mind and body, suggesting the idea of mind-body dualism. He believed the mind and body are separate, with the mind as the center of consciousness and the body as the tool for interacting with the world. This separation raises deep questions about existence and whether consciousness can exist beyond the body, impacting our views on the afterlife and places like Heaven (Andrade, n.d.).

As we think about these philosophical ideas, we start to see connections between ancient wisdom and modern questioning—between abstract thinking and deep existential inquiries. Although these philosophical systems may not prove Heaven in a scientific way, they encourage deep thinking and self-reflection.

In our search for knowledge, it's important to recognize that human experience and knowledge have many parts. Scientific evidence helps us comprehend the physical world, while philosophy helps us think about things beyond what we can touch, like questions about life, awareness, and going beyond the ordinary.

These philosophical thoughts lay the groundwork for contemplating the existence of higher realms such as Heaven. They prompt us to ponder the essence of reality and inquire whether there is more to existence beyond the visible and tangible.

Philosophy isn't enough for everyone. Our personal experiences also influence what we believe about the afterlife. Maybe you've had moments that felt special, like you were connected to something bigger than you. These moments could be seen as brief looks into Heaven—times when the line between our world and the divine seems to fade. We will explore many of these stories in Chapter 6.

Empirical evidence, usually linked to science, can also help us grasp the idea of Heaven. While it can't definitively prove Heaven's existence, it can give us insights into human experiences and consciousness. For example, studies on near-death experiences share stories of people encountering a realm beyond our world. Even though these experiences can't be measured in a typical way, they are important for exploring human consciousness and the potential for an afterlife.

When thinking about Heaven, it's important to keep an open mind and be ready to explore different perspectives. Whether through philosophy, personal thoughts, or scientific study, each way gives us a special view to ponder the mysteries of life after death.

As you think about these things, may you find peace and hope in the concept of a place where love, light, and transcendence are strong.

In our exploration, we've discussed that Heaven is not a far-off idea but a state of existence beyond what we know on Earth. It's a place of everlasting love, peace, and happiness, where all the hardships of this world turn into something wonderful and beyond.

As we conclude this chapter, it is time to delve deeper into the ways in which we can find comfort in the afterlife. I invite you to carry with you the knowledge that Heaven is not some distant dream but an essence of peace you can tap into when you are in need of hope, and that love endures beyond the boundaries of time and space.

CHAPTER 3:

Finding Comfort in the Afterlife

In this chapter, we delve into exploring the mysteries of the afterlife, to find comfort and healing after experiencing loss and grief. Many find peace in the idea of a Heaven: a place of beauty and love, where weary souls can rest and look forward to reuniting with loved ones.

For many years, and in different societies, people have found great comfort and hope in the idea of Heaven. It almost reassures us that death is not the final chapter but a path to a better place. In this realm, there is no more pain or sadness, and love is limitless.

Heaven is often seen as a powerful force that can heal deep emotional pain. Believing in an afterlife gives us strength, knowing our loved ones are waiting for us. This belief helps us face each day with hope, cherishing memories of those we've lost peacefully.

In this chapter, we will talk about how the idea of an afterlife brings comfort to people who are grieving. We will look at how believing in life after death can change how we see loss and help us make sense of pain. We will also share stories of people who have felt better by believing in the idea of a Heaven and an afterlife, showing how belief can really help us feel more at peace.

The Role of an Afterlife in Providing Peace When Grieving

When people have grim or unsure thoughts about what happens after we die, it can make dealing with loss even harder. Not knowing if there's an afterlife can make us feel like we're stuck in a cycle of intrusive, upsetting thoughts, similar to what people go through after a traumatic event. And for those who don't think they'll see their loved ones again after death, it often leads to more feelings of sadness, anger, and those intrusive thoughts for months after losing someone close.

Some experts think that believing in an afterlife can actually help us cope with the pain of losing someone we love, as well as ease our worries about our own mortality. For older adults who've lost a partner, these beliefs can be especially comforting, giving them a sense of purpose during tough times and keeping their emotional bond with their late spouse strong (Carr & Sharp, 2014).

Studies have shown that the idea of a traditional afterlife, where good people are rewarded and reunited with their loved ones, can actually help widowed spouses see their loss in a more positive light. It gives them a way to understand the death and come to terms with the fact that they'll also pass away someday. This way of thinking can soften the blow of grief, making it easier to handle the feelings of loss, separation, and sadness (Carr & Sharp, 2014).

When we face loss, it's like a storm that hits us with all sorts of questions about life, death, and what comes after. These aren't just everyday thoughts—they're the big, soul-searching kind that shake us to our core. But you know what? It's okay to wrestle with them. In fact, it can truly help with healing.

One of the things that spirituality often brings into focus is the idea of life after death. This belief can be incredibly comforting because it whispers to us that we might see our loved ones again someday. And it eases that fear of the unknown, especially when we're grappling with loss.

You know what else? Spirituality is all about connection. It's about feeling part of something bigger—whether it's the universe, a higher power, or simply being surrounded by a community who gets it. And that connection is like a warm hug for our souls when we're feeling lost and alone.

Oh, and let's not forget about the frameworks that spirituality offers for understanding loss. They give us answers to some of the hardest questions we face, like: *Why did we have to say goodbye? What happens next?* While they might not take away the pain entirely, they offer us some peace—some calm within the chaos.

We are aware of the countless spiritual paths out there, each with its own way of helping us through grief. Buddhism, for example, teaches us about impermanence and letting go, which can be incredibly freeing when we're mourning. Christianity, with its promise of eternal life, reminds us that love transcends even death itself.

If you don't have a belief in organized religion, there's still room for spirituality in your life. It might be found in nature, in moments of mindfulness, or simply in the quiet spaces where you can reflect and heal.

The bottom line is that grief and spirituality go hand in hand. They're like close friends who walk with us through the darkest times, offering comfort and companionship along the way. And however you choose to walk your path—whether it's steeped in tradition or forged from your own beliefs—remember that there's no right or wrong way to grieve. It's all about finding what brings you peace and healing as you move through the storm.

Exploring the Transformative Power of Belief in the Afterlife

Let's talk about the transformative power of belief in the afterlife. It's not about escaping the pain or pretending it doesn't exist; it's about finding a new perspective. When we believe in an afterlife—a realm where our loved ones exist in beauty and tranquility—it can bring a sense of peace to our hearts. Knowing that they're in a place where they are truly themselves, free from pain and suffering, can offer a profound comfort to us.

But how does this belief impact our own lives? It shifts our focus from the finality of death to the eternal nature of love. It reminds us that our existence here on earth is just one chapter in a much grander story. This realization can infuse our lives with a newfound appreciation for the present moment.

Imagine tasting flavors more vividly, seeing colors more vibrantly, and cherishing every sunset as if it were a masterpiece. By living in alignment with the belief in an afterlife, we learn to savor each moment. It's about finding beauty in the simple things, embracing life with open arms, and living each day with intention.

But embracing this perspective also requires us to acknowledge and accept our feelings—the positive and the negative. It's about being honest with ourselves and allowing ourselves to feel whatever emotions come up. Whether it's sadness, anger, or even moments of fleeting joy, each emotion is a testament to the depth of our love and connection.

Love becomes our guiding light in this journey. It's not just about expressing love toward others but also toward ourselves. Taking time each day to practice acts of kindness, both big and small, fosters a sense of connection and fulfillment. It's about being there for others, offering a listening ear, and extending grace and compassion to ourselves in moments of need.

Living a life with purpose becomes paramount. By identifying our passions and values, we can align our actions with our true desires. It's about pursuing what sets our souls on fire, whether it's through creative expression, meaningful work, or simply being present for those we care about.

But life is also about change and impermanence. Nothing stays the same forever, and learning to embrace the natural ebb and flow of life is essential. It's about letting go of attachments to outcomes, embracing new experiences, and finding beauty in the midst of uncertainty.

Lastly, cultivating a sense of spirituality adds depth and meaning to our lives. It's about connecting with something greater than ourselves—whether it's through meditation, prayer, or spending time in nature. This spiritual journey is deeply personal and doesn't necessarily adhere to any specific belief system. It's about finding what resonates with our souls and allowing it to guide us on our path.

A Discussion With Alison

What if there is an afterlife or a Heaven? What if it doesn't exist? How does our belief system impact our grief? When we lose a loved one, all we have are more questions. I think it's important to recognize that the unknown is going to be scary, impact our anxiety, and intensify our grief.

Belief affects us in a completely unique way. It can bring calm, peace, or leave us in a happy state of mind. When someone possesses knowledge—not necessarily proof—about a subject, it can provide a sense of understanding, confidence, and security. This knowledge may contribute to a feeling of being educated and capable of making informed decisions or engaging in meaningful discussions.

On the flip side, lacking information on a subject can evoke feelings of uncertainty, curiosity, or even anxiety. The lack of knowledge can generate a feeling of unease or a drive to find solutions and bridge the gaps in comprehension. Yet, it's crucial to recognize that being unaware of something doesn't always result in adverse outcomes. It can also nurture a sense of awe, receptiveness to learning, and the chance for exploration and revelation.

I recently sat down with my wife, Alison, to discuss the afterlife and the concept of Heaven. I frequently engage in these deep, meaningful conversations with her. Not only do they prove to be fascinating discussions, but they also bring us closer together. *I love you, Alison!*

We have both experienced the loss of parents in the past few years. I lost my father in November 2020, while Alison lost her father in October 2021 and her mother in June 2023. Our conversations often revolve around reminiscing about their kindness, love, and wisdom, which still resonate with us. Curious about Alison's perspective on Heaven, I presented her with a scenario to understand her thoughts. I would like to share the details of our conversation.

Picture a scenario where we all depart from Earth to live on the moon. In this hypothetical situation, your 97-year-old mother resides in a retirement home. The time comes for her to leave for the moon, and as you bid her farewell at the retirement home's entrance, you realize it's a final goodbye. With your mother's departure, unanswered questions about her journey to, arrival at, and well-being on the moon linger, leaving you with a sense of uncertainty.

Now let's envision the other scenario.

When your mother departs from the retirement home, you witness everything unfold. After saying goodbye, as she exits the facility, you watch—on a big screen—her progression to the launch pad, then into space and toward the moon. Witnessing her landing and transition to her new habitat, you find peace in her evident joy and well-being. Although communication is not possible, you find comfort in knowing her whereabouts and her contentment.

"Alison, could you describe the emotions you might experience in the first scenario versus the second? The first scenario involves saying goodbye to someone who is about to travel to the moon, leaving you with no contact or knowledge of their well-being. In contrast, the second scenario involves witnessing their journey, knowing they are happy and safe. Can you share your feelings and the distinctions between the two situations— the mix of the unknown, fear, sadness, love, and potential pain that you could endure?"

Alison thought about the situation before pointing out the differences; the difference between knowing and not knowing greatly affected her feelings: like night and day. Not knowing brought a lot of fear and anxiety. Having many unanswered questions was painful and made her cry. The uncertainty about the fate of someone she loved was especially upsetting in this case.

In the other scenario, witnessing her mother's journey to the moon, Alison expressed that she felt immense joy in the knowledge that her mother was safe and content, and that one day she would make the same journey to reunite with her, bringing her a sense of peace.

Understanding what happens after we die can help ease the pain of losing someone we love. But how do we gain this understanding? Where can we find answers? And how can we know if the information is true? We realize that ideas about Heaven vary, depending on personal beliefs and different religions and philosophies. People have been discussing and thinking about this topic for centuries.

Personal Stories of Finding Comfort Through the Concept of Heaven

Charlotte's Story

Charlotte's story is a poignant reminder of the deep bond between a grandmother and her granddaughter. Growing up, Charlotte shared countless precious moments with her grandmother: baking birthday cakes, going on weekend getaways, and learning life's lessons together. But when Charlotte was just 20 years old, their world was turned upside down by a devastating diagnosis: cancer.

Charlotte became her grandmother's unwavering support system throughout the grueling year of cancer treatments. From driving her to each appointment to holding her hand through the darkest moments, Charlotte was there every step of the way. Despite the pain and uncertainty, their bond only grew stronger.

The last Christmas they spent together was filled with unimaginable anguish. Charlotte watched helplessly as her grandmother suffered, her heart breaking with each passing day. And then, in the quiet of a cold December night, Charlotte found herself faced with the unimaginable reality of her grandmother's imminent departure.

As Charlotte rushed home for a brief respite, she couldn't shake the feeling of guilt gnawing at her heart. The weight of not being by her grandmother's side in her final moments threatened to consume her. Alone in her grief, Charlotte stood on the balcony, the bitter cold biting at her skin. And then, amid the swirling snowflakes and silent darkness, she witnessed a miraculous sight—a shooting star streaking across the sky.

For Charlotte, a devoted stargazer, this moment held a significance beyond words. In that fleeting instant, she felt a profound connection with her grandmother—a reassurance that she was not alone. It was a profound realization that her grandmother's presence transcended the physical realm, bringing comfort and peace to Charlotte's shattered heart.

In the days that followed, Charlotte navigated the blur of visitations and funeral preparations in a state of numbness. But in that pain and sorrow, she found a glimmer of hope—a newfound belief in the afterlife: a Heaven where her grandmother's spirit lived on. It was a revelation that brought her a sense of peace and understanding, turning her grief into a source of hope.

George's Story

George has experienced deep suffering, as many have likely experienced too. Losing a child causes unimaginable pain that affects one to the core, leaving them feeling lost and uncertain. However, even in the darkest moments, there remains a small sense of hope.

For George, it began as a feeling: a sense of impending doom that he chose to ignore until his life took unexpected turns. His wife endured two miscarriages, and three years later, they faced heartbreak with the devastating loss of their only child. Each event felt like fate was playing a cruel trick, leaving George shocked and unable to comprehend what was happening.

Amid this anguish, George found a source of hope. It wasn't a sudden or miraculous moment, but rather a calm and constant presence. Jesus walked with him through his toughest times, offering love and comfort amid the sadness.

When his daughter passed away, George struggled with his faith amidst the intense pain. Doubts arose, questioning why such a tragedy occurred. Despite feeling anger and turning away, George felt that God never abandoned him. God's love remained steadfast, providing stability to George during the mourning period.

Before his daughter's funeral, George reluctantly agreed to have her baptized. As the priest anointed her with oil, a sense of comfort mingled with the heaviness of his sadness. With hesitation, he lit a candle in the church and gazed up at the cross, grappling with why he was being subjected to such torment.

Then, he saw her. She appeared peaceful, with a serene smile adorning her angelic face, as if she were playing happily. George watched as she journeyed home to her final resting place.

Despite uncertainty about the future, George moves forward with a newfound sense of purpose. The trials he faced have changed him. While many questions remain unanswered and doubts linger, he has learned to relinquish the need for all the answers. Trusting in the invisible force that guides him, George has discovered a tranquil feeling that transcends the need for understanding.

Christine's Story

Christine grew up surrounded by illness and uncertainty. Her father, a paraplegic, frequented hospitals due to a car accident that left him paralyzed from the waist down at the age of 41, when Christine was just 15.

Now in her 40s, Christine reminisces more about her life with her father in a wheelchair than without one. As her father aged, health issues increasingly plagued him, a predictable progression that one can only brace for to a certain extent.

When Christine's mother decided she could no longer cope with the added stress and sought a divorce, Christine stepped up to take on full responsibility for his care—despite the fact that she was 32 years old, and married, with two young children. She never hesitated, driven by her deep love for her father and her desire to provide him with the best life possible, surrounded by family.

As her father neared 65, they shared late-night, profound conversations about life and death. Aware of the impending struggle Christine would face upon his passing, her father imparted a poignant analogy the night before his departure.

They discussed the evolution of societal attitudes towards life and death, noting how advancements in science and technology have prolonged life and lessened the fear of death. Yet, despite this, the reality of mortality remained. They talked about how people often live as if death is a disruption, failing to grasp its inherent nature in life.

It was during these discussions that Christine's father shared the analogy of cake in Heaven. He likened humans to slices of cake, each perfectly created by God—the master baker—from the same precise recipe, but unique in their own right.

Despite her father's penchant for science and fact-based inquiry, he always returned to the cake theory. Almost a year since his passing, Christine finds solace in recalling those conversations, especially the peace that would wash over her father's face when discussing the concept of baking that celestial cake.

On days when the longing for her father is most acute, Christine bakes a large chocolate cake; it's a tangible way to honor her emotions, her loss, and, above all, her father.

As Christine reflects on her journey through grief and the search for comfort in the afterlife, she hopes others may find solace in shared experiences and the understanding that while grief may endure, it can also foster strength and connection.

Within this chapter, we focused on finding comfort in an afterlife and what that means to those grieving. When we change our perspective and visualize our loved ones in a place of peace and love, our load of sorrow and pain lightens.

Up next, we will take a closer look at how different cultures and religions view Heaven as a whole. Are there different levels and realms to explore? Turn the page and walk this peaceful path of discovery with me.

CHAPTER 4:

Heavenly Realms

When we think about Heaven, we often wonder if it's just one big place where everyone goes or if there are different parts to it. It's not just a matter of curiosity, but it's about finding comfort and hope when we're grieving or feeling lost.

Think of Heaven like a huge mansion with many rooms, each with its own special beauty. Some rooms might be filled with light where kind-hearted people find peace, while others might be places of wisdom where seekers learn and grow.

As we try to understand Heaven, we're like explorers on a hike, looking beyond what we can see with our eyes. We wonder if our loved ones are in the same part of Heaven as us or if they're in different places that we can't see. This question can make our hearts ache with longing and uncertainty.

It's crucial we acknowledge that the beliefs concerning multiple realms or levels within Heaven can differ among various religious and spiritual traditions. The details and depictions of these realms may also vary, showcasing the distinct teachings and understandings of each belief system.

But as we search for answers, let's keep our hearts and minds open to the idea that Heaven is filled with love and compassion. Even though we may not be able to see our loved ones, we can trust that they're still with us, wrapped in the comforting embrace of divine love. In the following pages, we'll look deeper into the mysteries of Heaven's different realms.

Are There Different Realms in Heaven?

In the pages of the Bible, we find hints and whispers of the possibility of multiple realms in Heaven. Let's start with the writings of the apostle Paul in 2 Corinthians 12:2-4. What exactly does Paul mean when he starts to discuss a third heaven? In this part of the Bible, Paul tells his own story of going to Heaven. It seems he paints quite the picture of being caught up to the "third heaven" and how he heard "inexpressible things" (*What Does 2 Corinthians*, n.d.).

Let's break it down a bit more. The full quote is as follows (*King James Bible*, 2017/1769):

I knew a man in Christ above fourteen years ago, (whether in the body, I cannot tell; or whether out of the body, I cannot tell: God knoweth;) such an one caught up to the third heaven. And I knew such a man, (whether in the body, or out of the body, I cannot tell: God knoweth;) How that he was caught up into paradise, and heard unspeakable words, which it is not lawful for a man to utter. (2 Corinthians 12:2–4)

The term "heavens" can be used to describe many places. We have to consider that it is being used to signify the sky or earth's atmosphere, which is often referenced as the "first heaven."

It is also quoted as the outer space, where the stars and planets are known as the second Heaven. "For the stars of heaven and their constellations will not flash forth their light; The sun will be dark when it rises and the moon will not shed its light" (*New American Standard Bible*, 1995/1971, Isaiah 13:10).

It can also mean the place above the other levels of heaven where God lives—a place referred to as "the third heaven" and taken from various verses, including Isaiah 66:1 (*King James Bible*, 2017/1769) which states "Thus saith the LORD, The heaven is my throne, and the earth is my footstool: where is the house that ye build unto me? and where is the place of my rest?"

When Paul mentions going to the third Heaven, we can assume he is referring to the location where God resides.

Pause and think about this idea: Just like we see different landscapes on Earth, could there be various beautiful and majestic places in Heaven? Imagine heavenly levels crafted from different architecture, each revealing a unique aspect of divine beauty and glory.

And let's not forget the words of Jesus himself, recorded in the Gospel of John. In John 14:2, Jesus speaks of his Father's house, proclaiming, "In my Father's house are many rooms" (*The Holy Bible: King James Version [KJV]*, 2011/1611). Now, this imagery of many rooms or dwelling places has sparked wonder and speculation among scholars and seekers alike. Could these *rooms* signify distinct realms or areas within the heavenly abode, each prepared with meticulous care and overflowing with love?

As we read these passages, it's important to approach them with respect and modesty, knowing that our knowledge of the afterlife is limited. Even though we may not fully understand, we can still feel blessed and curious. Thinking about various heavenly realms encourages us to expand our view, appreciate the vastness of divine secrets, and find comfort in the belief that there is a world of endless opportunities and everlasting peace beyond our earthly lives.

The Seven Skies—Islam

In Islam, Heaven is known as *Jannah*: a paradise where good individuals go after they pass away. Described in the holy

Quran as "gardens of pleasure," it is where people receive rewards for their good deeds in life. By following Allah's rules, avoiding sin, and being good, one is believed to enter Heaven. Islam teaches that there are seven levels of Heaven, each with unique features and a different prophet occupying them. Let's have a closer look at those now (Ayoub, 2021b):

1. *Jannat-al-Adan*: The eternal place is where a Muslim goes after repenting for their sins. In *Surah Tawbah*, Allah promises believers a place in the Gardens of Adan, where they receive great acceptance from Allah and find everything they desire from the flowing rivers below.

2. *Jannat-al-Firdaws*: This is a garden filled with various plants, including grapevines. It is the highest and most superior level, surpassing all other levels in *Kutub-i-Sitta*.

3. *Jannat-an-Naim*: In *Surah Yunus*, it is mentioned that those who believe in Allah and do good deeds will remain steadfast in goodness throughout their lives. These faithful individuals will encounter rivers flowing beneath them in the Paradise of Delight and will be elevated to a level constructed from iron.

4. *Jannat-ul-Mawa*: It is a brass sanctuary for devoted individuals and martyrs. *Mawa* is a place of shelter with houses and residences. *Surah An Najm* mentions this place as the Garden of Adobe for those seeking refuge. It is located near a lote tree on the edge of Heaven.

5. *Dar-ul-Khuld*: This level, known as the Garden of Immortality, grants eternal life. It is reserved for those who stay dedicated to their path without straying, offering solace for the challenges faced on the journey and marking the end of the voyage.

6. **Dar-ul-Maqaam:** A fundamental aspect of one's being, this place is where the soul discovers a permanent sanctuary. In *Surah al Fatir*, this heavenly stage is described as a secure haven where all pain and weariness disappear, shielding the soul from any disturbances.

7. **Dar-us-Salam:** It is a place of well-being known as the seventh level of Heaven, where safety and peace reside. In *Surah al Yunus*, Allah calls back those destined to follow the Straight Path, and in *Surah al An'am*, He refers to it as a place of His protection.

Some scholars believe in the existence of the eighth level of Heaven known as *Illiyyun*. It is believed to be a place for devout believers and is guarded by the *Hafaza* angels who protect souls. It is said to be where people receive rewards for their good deeds. In Islamic belief, there are differing views on the number of levels in Heaven, with some suggesting a hundred levels. These planes are thought to represent different ranks or grades. Another interpretation of the hundred levels is that they symbolize the various degrees of *Jannah* where believers are placed based on their actions. It is assumed that the distance between these levels increases as one ascends (Ayoub, 2021b).

28 Levels of Heaven—Buddhism

Many religions, including Buddhism, believe in Heaven and Hell. Buddhism teaches that Heaven is divided into twenty-eight levels. The twenty-eight heavens are divided into three realms: the *desire* realm with six levels of Heaven, the *form* realm with eighteen levels of Heaven, and the *formless* realm with four levels of Heaven (Sheng Yen, 2007, p. 41).

Let's take a journey through the realms of Heaven as understood in Buddhism. These celestial dimensions offer insight into realms of existence beyond our ordinary perception, realms that hold mysteries and lessons for us all.

The Desire Realm: The Six Heavens

In the desire realm, there are six heavens where beings live lives much like we do. They have bodies much like humans, with physical needs and desires for sustenance and pleasure. These beings only indulge in the joys of food, drink, and other sensory pleasures, hence the term "desire" realm. Yet, within the six heavens of the desire realm, five other domains exist—the human realm, the asura realm, the animal realm, the hungry ghost realm, and the Hell realm—each with its own experiences and challenges (Buddhist Cosmology, n.d.).

The Form Realm: The Eighteen Heavens

Moving beyond the desire realm, we enter the form realm, where eighteen heavens await. Here, beings transcend the desires that bind us in the material world. They no longer find joy or a need for food, intimacy, or drink. They are now superior to humans in spirituality, community, and beauty. They are fueled by the bliss of meditation as we are by food (Buddhist Cosmology, n.d.).

The Formless Realm: The Four Heavens

In these realms, beings have moved beyond physical form completely, existing only as spiritual entities. Released from the limitations of the physical world, they dwell in states of pure consciousness and bliss. They have zero attachment to the constraints of appearance and are not limited by the need for intimate pleasure or food (Buddhist Cosmology, n.d.).

Even in the beauty of the heavens, Buddhism teaches us that they are still places of confusion. Even Heavenly beings must go through being born and dying, unable to avoid the basic suffering that comes with existence. However, there is hope. According to Buddhism, we can break free from this cycle by reaching nirvana. Nirvana is the highest form of liberation, providing total freedom from suffering and the continuous cycle of rebirth.

Sakra-Devanamin-Indra, also called Lord Indra, rules the Heaven of the Thirty-Three Gods, a significant place in Buddhist stories. In this Heaven, the Buddha taught his mother, Queen Maya, as a gesture of respect and love. In this Heavenly realm, creatures experience joys that are impossible for us to imagine. They glow with light, move freely through the skies, and live in eternal happiness and wealth. Their lives are incredibly long, much longer than ours (Buddhist Cosmology, n.d.) .

Buddhism teaches us that achieving rebirth in Heaven, although appealing, is not the final objective. It is attained through numerous virtuous deeds and merits gathered throughout multiple lifetimes. Moving beyond heavenly realms, the ultimate aim is to seek nirvana, the genuine freedom from suffering.

In Buddhism, Heaven is just one part of existence. It provides rewards and challenges, reminding us that being good and compassionate can lead to higher states of being. Even in the midst of suffering, there is hope for transcendence.

As we ponder the mysteries of Heaven, let us also reflect on our own lives and actions. May we cultivate virtue, compassion, and wisdom, knowing that each step on this journey brings us closer to understanding and liberation.

Does My Present Role Affect My Role in Heaven?

Have you ever thought about the timeless question: *How do I get to Heaven?* This question reflects a desire within us for something greater than our earthly lives. Maybe, like the rich young ruler in Matthew 19:16–26 (*The Bible: English Standard Version [ESV]*, 2016/2001), you've struggled with this question, trying to find the answer to enter Heaven or take peace in knowing your loved ones that have passed are there now.

In our quest for answers, we often turn to the teachings of various religions and philosophies, all of which extol the virtues of goodness and righteousness. Be a good person, follow the commandments, and live by the Golden Rule—these are the common refrains that echo across diverse belief systems. And yet, is this truly the heart of Christianity? Is being a good person the ticket to Heaven?

Join me as we explore a significant conversation in the Bible between Jesus and a sincere seeker, the wealthy young ruler. The young man asks a meaningful question: "What must I do to have eternal life?" Like many, he thought following rules and being good would guarantee his spot in Heaven. However, Jesus, with great insight, reveals a profound truth beyond mere human effort. Jesus probes the young man's understanding, challenging the very premise upon which his question rests. For in the economy of Heaven, goodness is not a currency we can amass through our own efforts. No one is truly good except God alone. The young man's earnest declaration of keeping the commandments since his youth reveals not his righteousness, but his blindness to the true nature of the law and his own inadequacy (*What Does Matthew 19:16 Mean?*, n.d.).

The bible tells us that Jesus then compassionately reveals to the young man that his love for wealth was like an idol, stopping him from fully committing to follow Christ. It's a wake-up call that simply being a good person in society's eyes isn't sufficient. Our goodness is flawed, influenced by sin, and doesn't meet God's standards completely. The amazing news that goes beyond human efforts and worthiness is that salvation is not something we earn for being good; It is a gift given to us out of love by Jesus Christ. Even when we were still sinning, Christ died for us, connecting our sinful nature with God's holiness (*Why Is Being a Good,* 2022).

Christianity believes that salvation is not something we earn by being good, but it's a gift we receive by believing in what Jesus did on the cross. It's available to everyone who is willing to admit their mistakes, turn away from their sins, and trust Jesus as their leader and rescuer. Only through Jesus can we be made right with God and enter Heaven, as He is the ultimate example of goodness and the one who paid for our wrongdoings with His sacrifice.

In the depths of grief, it can be easy to lose sight of this eternal truth. We may find ourselves consumed by questions and doubts, wondering if our loved ones have truly found peace in the arms of the divine. Yet, it is in these moments of uncertainty that faith whispers to our hearts, reminding us of the promises that await us in the heavenly realms.

Heaven is not merely a distant realm shrouded in mystery; it is a place of unimaginable beauty and joy, where the souls of the departed find rest and fulfillment in the presence of God. It is a place where pain and sorrow are no more, where tears are replaced with smiles, and where love exists.

When we anchor our hearts in this hope, we find relief from the weight of our grief. For we know that our loved ones are not lost to us forever, but merely waiting for us on the other side of eternity. Their spirits live on in the embrace of divine love.

This perspective of Heaven offers us respite from our grief, reminding us that death is not the end, but merely a transition to a higher plane of existence. It invites us to trust in the unfathomable wisdom of the divine, knowing that all things work together for good for those who love and believe in God and Heaven.

Judgment Day

Death is something that happens to everyone, no matter who they are. People have different beliefs about what happens after death. In Islam, it is believed that life continues after death in the hereafter.

Society is so focused on living that we often overlook the reality of death. Our busy lives, cozy homes, and relationships consume our time, leaving little room for contemplating life's transience.

Sudden events, like a loved one getting sick or a sudden loss, can make us confront the truth of our lives. Feeling powerless, we are reminded of how fragile life is, causing us to rethink our values and how we live.

Muslims believe that Allah determines when a person dies. After death, they are believed to stay in their graves until the Day of Judgment, also known as Yawm al-din. On this day, Allah evaluates them based on their actions during their life. The deceased will be raised from their graves and presented before Allah for judgment. This concept is known as the resurrection of the body (Ayoub, 2021a).

People who do good things in their life go to Paradise, where there is no pain, illness, or sorrow. On the other hand, those who do bad things go to Hell, where they suffer physically and spiritually. However, Muslims believe that not all bad deeds are punished because Allah is forgiving. He forgives those who lament what they've done and have done specific good works in their lives (Ayoub, 2021a).

As a result, death is not seen as the end but as a transition to an eternal existence. Muslims believe in the one God who created and sustains the universe. They seek guidance to understand a reality that is beyond what humans can see. This advice is derived from the examples set by prophets and the teachings contained in holy books. Throughout the ages, prophets—such as Noah, Moses, Adam, Abraham, Jesus, and Muhammad (the last prophet)—were sent by God. Additionally, God revealed sacred texts, such as the Torah, the Gospel, and the Quran.

The belief is those who have achieved their life's purpose and lived with goodness will go to a never-ending paradise filled with happiness. In this heavenly place, they will live in stunning homes, free from tiredness, illness, and aging. God will take away all negativity and suffering, bringing complete healing and creating a world of plenty, luxury, beautiful gardens, and flowing rivers. People who disobey God or harm others will go to Hell. They didn't follow God's guidance despite His blessings. Hell, as described in the Quran, is a place of intense suffering, extreme heat, thirst, and fire (*Belief in Judgement Day*, 2014).

It is taught that God wants each of us to be saved in the afterlife. He has given guidance and signs for those who search for Him and think about His teachings. We can choose to enjoy the world freely or follow His rules.

It is stated in the Quran, "Why should God make you suffer torment if you are thankful and believe in Him? God always rewards gratitude and He knows everything" (T*he Qur'an*, 2004, 4:147).

In Islam it is taught that life is seen as a test to decide where we'll end up in the afterlife. People who grasp this believe that what happens after death depends on how they live now. They appreciate the blessings from God, worship humbly, and spread goodness. By living this way, they find a deeper purpose beyond just seeking pleasure in this world.

Muslims believe that God is fair and keeps a detailed record of everything we do. In the afterlife, we will be rewarded or punished based on our actions in this life, where true justice is upheld. In the Quran God states (The Qur'an, 2004):

> Do those who commit evil deeds really think that We will deal with them in the same way as those who believe and do righteous deeds, that they will be alike in their living and their dying? How badly they judge! (45:21)

As we conclude our journey through the ethereal realms of Heaven, I hope you find calm in the beauty and wonder that awaits us beyond this earth. We've explored the notion that Heaven is not a singular destination but a multilayered level of existence, each realm offering its own unique essence and purpose.

From the celestial realms, where souls bask in the pure radiance of divine love—to the realms of learning and growth, where knowledge and enlightenment are eternal pursuits—we've glimpsed the boundless possibilities that await us in the afterlife.

But within these varied realms, one truth remains constant: Heaven is a place of love, compassion, and infinite grace. It is a sanctuary where our souls find rest and renewal, where our deepest longings are fulfilled, and where the mysteries of existence are finally revealed.

As we prepare to look closer into the sacred texts, spiritual beliefs, and wisdom of the ages in the next chapter, let us carry with us the understanding that Heaven is not just a distant hope but a present reality.

In the pages that follow, we will draw inspiration from the insights of renowned spiritual leaders and philosophers, explore the mystical traditions that offer glimpses into the nature of Heaven, and discover the practices and rituals that connect us with the divine realm.

CHAPTER 5:

Scripture, Spiritual Beliefs, and the Afterlife

The question that troubles us deeply is: *Where do our loved ones go after they die and will I be reunited with them?* This question has been asked throughout history, making us long for answers and a connection that goes beyond death.

In our search for answers, we are attracted to the various spiritual teachings and philosophies that shape human consciousness. Throughout different cultures and time periods, from the wisdom of ancient sages to the words of modern mystics, we sense a realm beyond what we can perceive. It's a place where love goes beyond time and space, and souls discover peace in eternity.

In Heaven, we are encouraged to explore different ideas that come from our imagination. This includes visions from religious beliefs and the creative works of poets and philosophers. Heaven's beauty and endless possibilities are waiting for us to discover and see those we love once again.

How do we find our way through so many different beliefs and thoughts? What do we do when we're unsure and confused about what lies ahead?

We can find the answers we are looking for not just in old books or religious buildings but, also, in moments of quiet thinking and listening to our hearts. Let's explore this together by letting go of strict beliefs and embracing the endless possibilities of our curiosity.

Will I See My Loved One Again?

Will we reunite with our beloved departed ones in the afterlife? It's a question that often finds its answer within belief and experiences.

In our exploration, we'll find that the response to this question is as varied as the colors of a sunset. Many faiths offer a resounding affirmation, comforting their followers with the promise of reunion beyond this earthly realm. And then there are those remarkable accounts from medical professionals who've stood witness to near-death experiences, with narratives that whisper of glimpses into realms where loved ones await.

We'll delve deeper into these fascinating accounts in an entire chapter devoted to near-death experiences, where stories of profound encounters may offer reassurance and stir the embers of hope within us. Yet, what we ultimately believe is deeply rooted in our individual belief systems, shaped by the experiences and convictions that define us.

Let's look at various religions and philosophies to understand different perspectives on reuniting after death. Through this exploration, may we find comfort and hope to help us cope with loss and deepen our understanding of love's enduring connection beyond life.

What the Bible Says About Reuniting With Loved Ones

Let me share with you words of comfort and assurance from the scriptures. In 1 Thessalonians 4:13-18, it beautifully captures the essence of hope that we find in our Christian faith. It says (*The Bible: ESV*, 2016/2001):

But we do not want you to be uninformed, brothers, about those who are asleep, that you may not grieve as others do who have no hope. For since we believe that Jesus died and rose again, even so, through Jesus, God will bring with him those who have fallen asleep. For this we declare to you by a word from the Lord, that we who are alive, who are left until the coming of the Lord, will not precede those who have fallen asleep. For the Lord himself will descend from Heaven with a cry of command, with the voice of an archangel, and with the sound of the trumpet of God. And the dead in Christ will rise first. Then we who are alive, who are left, will be caught up together with them in the clouds to meet the Lord in the air, and so we will always be with the Lord. Therefore encourage one another with these words. (1 Thessalonians 4:13-18)

These words are like a gentle embrace from above, assuring us that God will come for us, and in that glorious moment, we will be reunited with our beloved ones who have gone before us. Isn't that a comforting thought? It's a promise that transcends the boundaries of time and space, affirming that our bonds of love are eternal.

And then there's John 14:1-3, where Jesus tenderly assures us (*The Bible: ESV*, 2016/2001):

Let not your hearts be troubled. Believe in God; believe also in me. In my Father's house are many rooms. If it were not so, would I have told you that I go to prepare a place for you? And if I go and prepare a place for you, I will come again and will take you to myself, that where I am you may be also (John 14:1-3)

These words offer comfort to our weary hearts, painting a picture of a loving Father who has prepared a special place for each one of us in His eternal home.

Think about the idea of an afterlife like Jesus mentioned. He talks about getting a place ready for us in his Father's house, suggesting that our sense of self and connections with loved ones could continue even after we die. It's a comforting hint that the love we share might go beyond death.

Moreover, in the sacred verses of 1 Corinthians 15:42-44, we see the promise of glorified bodies at the resurrection. These may bear the imprints of our earthly journey, carrying with them the cherished memories and connections we had with our beloved family members (*The Bible: ESV*, 2016/2001).

And in the simple story of the wealthy man and Lazarus (*King James Bible*, 2017/1769, Luke 16:19-31), we see glimpses of remembrance, suggesting a continuity of awareness that spans the realms of existence.

While the Bible doesn't say for sure if we'll remember our loved ones in Heaven, it makes us think about the chance of being reunited. In Heaven, our idea of family is based on our spiritual family in Christ, which is the most important bond. Even though it might be different from our earthly relationships, the "feeling" of connection stays the same.

Religious Leaders and Scholars

Many great religious leaders are responsible for theories about this very topic. When we lose a loved one and those questions begin to wash over us, answers initiated by any of them may be found.

Muhammad, Prophet of Islam

Born in 570 C.E. in the bustling city of Mecca, Muhammad's journey unfolded with the weight of divine revelations upon his shoulders. Through the Qur'an, Islam's sacred scripture, his recitations became the cornerstone of a monotheistic tradition that echoes through the ages. At the age of 40, Muhammad embraced his role as a messenger of God, navigating the tumultuous landscape of political and military strife in Medina. With strategic acumen and steadfast faith, he forged alliances and led campaigns that reshaped the Arabian Peninsula, paving the way for the spread of Islam (Marks, 2024).

While history tells of conflicts and controversies, it also shows Muhammad's efforts for peace and reconciliation. In a turbulent era, Islam became a source of hope, providing comfort to the tired and direction to the confused.

Muslims believe that after death, souls reunite in the afterlife as Allah desires, regardless of where their physical bodies are buried. Time and space do not limit the connection between souls. Just like in life, where hearts can be close but different in nature, souls in the afterlife come together if they have a connection, or move apart if they don't. Happy souls, free from earthly worries, move through Paradise, meeting loved ones and sharing stories of their life journey (*Do the Souls Meet*, 2009).

For good and righteous people, the afterlife is a happy reunion with virtuous friends. But those suffering in torment are too consumed by their pain to join the happy gathering of the blessed. In the divine order, souls are connected by their shared deeds and dreams. As we explore Heaven's mysteries, we find comfort in the idea that love goes beyond life and death, creating an everlasting bond of connection and reunion (*Do the Souls Meet*, 2009).

Rishabhanatha

Considered a wise and enlightened figure in Jainism, *Rishabhanatha*—the first Tirthankara—lived long ago, guiding people toward knowledge and personal development. His teachings continue to resonate, providing us with wisdom about life's meaning and the journey to freedom. Legend tells the story of *Rishabhanatha*—highlighting his noble deeds, selfless teachings, and journey to enlightenment. His tale embodies sacrifice, devotion, and transcendence, showcasing the timeless pursuit of spiritual awakening (Marks, 2024).

But what does Jainism say about meeting our loved ones after death? In the intricate cosmology of Jain belief, the universe is not just a fleeting illusion but a profound expression of existence itself. It's a realm where living souls and non-living entities coexist, bound by the threads of karma and rebirth. Jains envision the universe as a vast space, comprised of five distinct realms. From the heavenly homes of wise beings to the earthly world of humans, each realm has its own importance in the overall creation. (Johnson, 2021).

Death, in Jainism, is not an end but a transition—a gateway to the next phase of existence. Through rituals like *sallekhana*, Jains prepare themselves for the inevitable passage, embracing the cycle of birth and rebirth with grace and acceptance (Johnson, 2021).

For Jains, death is not the end. It's a stop on the soul's journey. Reincarnation gives souls the opportunity to grow, learn, and eventually break free from karma's cycle. Deliverance, the highest spiritual achievement, is for souls who have let go of karma and found enlightenment. *Siddhas*, liberated souls, live in the Supreme Abode, a place of pure joy beyond earthly desires (Johnson, 2021).

In Jainism, liberated souls inspire followers to strive for perfection. These wise beings, though God-like, don't interfere in human lives but offer hope and remind us of our own potential.

Maimonides

Picture Maimonides, a wise and caring figure born in the 12th century. He is known for his important book, the Mishneh Torah, which shows his deep knowledge of Jewish law and tradition. In his writings, we discover valuable insights into life's mysteries. Maimonides was not just a scholar; he excelled in many areas like philosophy, history, science, and medicine. His intelligence influenced not only the Jewish community but, also, had an impact in Islamic regions. However, his life was full of challenges, leading him to make the difficult decision to leave his home in Córdoba and move to Egypt (Marks, 2024).

As we explore what Jewish tradition says about life after death, we find comfort in old customs that have lasted for generations. Visiting the graves of loved ones and including their spirits in family events show the strong connection between the living and the deceased. In Jewish mysticism, as shown in the *Zohar*, we see a place where our ancestors' souls celebrate our life achievements, showing a lasting connection beyond life and death (Kara-Ivanov Kaniel, 2019).

Yet, Judaism, with its focus on the sanctity of life in the present moment, leaves ample room for personal interpretation regarding the afterlife. Orthodox Jews may envision a heavenly abode for the righteous, a cycle of reincarnation, or await the dawn of messianic redemption for reunion and resurrection.

The Torah, the guiding light through the ages, offers glimpses of a future where the righteous are reunited with their loved ones, while the wicked face spiritual consequences. The concept of being "gathered to their people" transcends the physical realm, hinting at a deeper truth beyond mortal understanding (Rich, n.d.).

And yet, within the sacred texts, there exists the notion of *kareit*, spiritual excision, where certain sins lead to the soul's separation from the "World to Come." It is a sobering reminder of the delicate balance between free will and divine justice, woven into the essence of our being (Rich, n.d.).

Theological and Philosophical Literature

Let's explore the extensive world of theological and philosophical writings, where scholars and thinkers have been studying the mysteries of Heaven and the afterlife for centuries.

One interesting thing about these writings is that they offer a variety of perspectives, showing different aspects of important questions.

Take, for instance, the works of theologians like Thomas Aquinas. He was a significant figure in medieval Scholasticism, known for blending faith-based theological beliefs with philosophical reasoning. He was a respected authority in the Roman Catholic Church and a prolific writer. Aquinas passed away on March 7, 1274, at the Cistercian monastery of Fossanova in Italy (*Saint Thomas Aquinas*, 2023).

After finishing his studies, Aquinas dedicated himself to a life of traveling, writing, teaching, and preaching. Both religious institutions and universities sought to benefit from his wisdom, often referring to him as "The Christian Apostle" (*Saint Thomas Aquinas*, 2023).

During the medieval period, there was a big debate about how to blend faith and reason. People struggled to connect what they learned through religious teachings with what they observed and reasoned through their own senses. Averroes' "theory of the double truth" suggested that these two kinds of knowledge were completely opposite. However, Saint Thomas Aquinas disagreed. He believed that both faith and reason ultimately come from God and can work together. According to him, revelation can guide reason and prevent errors, while reason can help clarify and explain faith. His writings explore how faith and reason play roles in understanding and proving the existence of God and an afterlife.

On the other hand, philosophers like Plato and Immanuel Kant approach the topic from a more abstract angle. They ponder the nature of the soul, the concept of immortality, and the possibility of an afterlife beyond religious dogma. Their insights challenge us to think beyond the confines of conventional belief systems and explore the infinite possibilities of existence.

What's amazing is the variety of ideas shared by different voices. Some focus on faith and redemption, while others prioritize reason and rationality. Some see Heaven as a place of eternal joy, while others view it as a state of spiritual enlightenment beyond time and space. What is comforting is most believe we will see our loved ones again.

Personal Reflection and Contemplation

In the turbulent time of grief, it's crucial to find moments of stillness to carve a path of personal reflection and contemplation.

When we confront the question of life after death, it's like standing at the edge of an infinite abyss, peering into the unknown. Will we meet our loved ones again? Will there be calm beyond the veil of mortality? These are questions that echo within the chambers of our hearts, seeking answers that seem elusive in the haze of sorrow.

But with the uncertainty, there lies a profound opportunity for introspection. It's a chance to explore the recesses of our own beliefs, values, and experiences. Take a moment to sit with your thoughts, sift through the fragments of your soul, and unearth the truths that resonate within you. Your journey of self-awareness begins with understanding how your personal convictions shape your perception of the afterlife.

Engage in the pursuit of knowledge. Let the wisdom of ancient texts, philosophical treatises, and cultural narratives be your guiding stars. Immerse yourself in the human spirituality, exploring the myriad perspectives that come together to form a collective understanding.

Contemplate the existential questions that linger at the fringes of consciousness. What is the nature of existence? What is the purpose of life? And what lies beyond the threshold of death? These questions are not just for thinking, but they ask us to consider the very core of our being.

And as you ponder, remember to seek different perspectives. Have conversations with those whose beliefs differ from your own, because through this dialogue we expand the horizons of our understanding. Embrace the richness of human experience, honoring the various ways in which people perceive the mysteries of Heaven and the afterlife.

Set aside time to reflect and meditate. Be still and listen to your inner voice among the noise of the world. Use quiet time, writing, or mindfulness to explore and discover yourself.

And if you take comfort in the teachings of a specific faith, don't be afraid to ask for advice from fellow believers. Allow the wisdom of spiritual leaders to guide you like lanterns, showing you the way with their understanding and kindness.

But most importantly, when thinking about Heaven and the afterlife, keep an open heart and mind. Everyone's understanding of these mysteries is personal and influenced by their life experiences. Appreciate the different viewpoints in the world, as they show the endless complexity of human beliefs.

In your quest for understanding, may you find not just answers, but peace. And may the journey of personal reflection and contemplation lead you to a place of healing and hope within your grief.

CHAPTER 6:

Near Death Experiences and Reconnecting With Departed Loved Ones

...◈...

In this chapter, we look into one of the most intriguing phenomena surrounding the afterlife: near-death experiences (NDEs). These extraordinary encounters offer a glimpse into realms beyond our understanding—providing comfort, hope, and, sometimes, even profound transformation to those who experience them.

But what exactly is an NDE? It is a remarkable event that occurs when people, usually facing death because of illness or trauma, describe extraordinary perceptions and sensations. These can include feelings of peace, encounters with deceased loved ones, out-of-body experiences, and traveling through tunnels of light.

The experiences shared by people who have had near-death experiences vary widely. Some talk about seeing bright light, meeting angels or loved ones who have passed away. Many feel deep love and acceptance, and lose their fear and worries about earthly matters.

Interestingly, there are parallels between the accounts of NDEs and the descriptions of the afterlife found in various religious texts. Themes of light, love, and reunion with loved ones echo across cultures and belief systems, suggesting a universal truth underlying these experiences.

So, where does this leave us in our quest to understand the mysteries of Heaven? For many, the existence of NDEs serves as compelling evidence of an afterlife—a realm beyond the physical constraints of our earthly existence. If people can journey to the brink of death, glimpse the beauty and wonder of the beyond, and return to share their experiences, how can we not believe in the existence of something greater than ourselves?

What Are Near-Death Experiences

Often described as moments that some people report after they've come close to death or faced a life-threatening situation., they're pretty profound and can be truly transformative, involving a whole mix of sensations, perceptions, and emotions.

What's interesting is that these experiences are not restricted to specific groups of people. They have been reported by priests, ministers, doctors, scientists, adults, children, and even people who don't adhere to any specific religious beliefs. These experiences occur worldwide, transcending cultural differences and belief systems.

Near-death experiences happen when someone's in such a critical state that they're usually unconscious, in a coma, or even clinically declared dead. From a medical and logical standpoint, it doesn't quite add up, does it? I mean, how can someone who's out cold suddenly have these super clear, organized experiences that they can recall later?

Take cardiac arrest, for example. Typically, within 10–20 seconds after it happens, there's no significant measurable brain activity. So, logically speaking, having a vivid, detailed experience during this time should be pretty much impossible. Yet, many people who've had NDEs report exactly that (Long, 2014).

It's like they're tapping into some sort of supernormal consciousness when they're supposed to be out for the count. And what's even more curious is that they often remember these experiences despite the usual memory loss that comes with recovering from such a critical state.

Common Elements Reported in NDEs

Imagine a soul leaving its body and watching from above, showing the separation of soul and body but their lasting connection.

Then comes the tunnel, a pathway glowing with heavenly light, inviting the traveler to continue a voyage into the unfamiliar, yet strangely recognizable. Souls move through this bright passage, pulled by a mysterious power toward a destination shrouded in the indescribable beauty of the afterlife.

As the journey continues, the traveler feels an overwhelming sense of peace that goes beyond what we can normally understand on Earth. This peace is so deep that it overcomes any fear or doubt, wrapping the soul in a comforting embrace and sharing stories of everlasting comfort.

The life review is like a movie made of memories. Each memory is a piece of the soul's journey, unfolding before the person. Important moments from life are shown, highlighting the path taken and the lessons learned.

In the afterlife, souls meet loved ones, guides, and celestial beings—showing how all souls are connected in the grand scheme of existence.

In this world beyond what we can touch, our understanding goes beyond our bodies. Our senses become sharper, colors appear brighter, and we are more aware of the vast universe around us.

Despite the temptation of exploring beyond, there comes a time when the traveler must return to the earthly realm. This return is filled with challenges but also hope, leading to renewal and rebirth.

Recent studies on near-death experiences have found striking similarities among people who have crossed the threshold of death. Research from the Journal of Near-Death Studies shows that 4–8% of people have had these shared experiences (Oberhaus, 2017).

A new study from Belgium looked at 154 stories of near-death experiences. It found that 80% of people felt deep peace, 69% saw a bright light, and 64% encountered spirits or celestial beings (Oberhaus, 2017). These shared experiences go beyond time and space.

Research and Theories

In the field of science, researchers are continuously studying NDEs to understand human consciousness and the mysteries of existence. They use various methods like brain imaging and psychological tests to uncover the reasons and significance of these intense experiences. Their goal is to explore the physical, mental, and spiritual aspects of NDEs.

Some researchers believe that NDEs could be caused by the brain's reaction to trauma or lack of oxygen, leading to intense feelings and perceptions. Others study the complex interaction of chemicals and brain pathways to understand how the mind and body connect during these profound moments. Despite scientific investigation, mysteries remain, prompting us to contemplate the deeper meaning of these experiences (Lichfield, 2015).

NDEs give us a glimpse into the human mind, showing us what lies deep in our subconscious and our strong desire for something beyond the ordinary. These experiences, which can include meeting heavenly figures and reliving our lives, have a big impact on how we grow personally and spiritually. They push us to face our fears, recognize the endless possibilities within us, and rethink what we know about life, death, and everything in between.

Spiritually, NDEs resonate deeply with those who view them through a lens of faith and mysticism. For many, these encounters serve as sacred glimpses into the divine realms, affirming the eternal nature of the soul and the loving presence of a higher power. Across cultures and creeds, NDEs bear witness to the ineffable beauty of the afterlife, offering peace to the grieving and hope to the weary traveler on life's journey.

Despite lots of research and human experiences, scientists and academics still argue. Some doubt near-death experiences, saying they are just hallucinations or brain activity before death. Others struggle to understand consciousness, thinking about mysteries that science can't explain.

Ultimately, whether one chooses to believe in the accounts of those who have experienced NDEs is a deeply personal decision, shaped by one's own beliefs, experiences, and perspectives. Some may find comfort in the certainty of scientific explanations, while others may draw peace from the timeless wisdom of spiritual traditions. Yet, in the end, what truly matters is the profound impact these experiences have on the lives of those who undergo them—offering hope, love, and understanding in the darkness of uncertainty.

Ernest Hemingway, who experienced war and death firsthand, later incorporated his near-death encounter into his writing. In his story *The Snows of Kilimanjaro,* he describes a soul leaving the body in a way that reflects a classic NDE: darkness, relief from pain, and moving toward a bright light symbolizing peace (Koch, 2020).

NDEs come in varying shades. Some paint a picture of overwhelming serenity—a connection to something divine. Yet, not all journeys to the brink of death are bathed in light. Some are shrouded in darkness, haunted by fear and despair.

In 1791, British admiral Sir Francis Beaufort nearly drowned, an experience he later recounted in this manner (Koch, 2020):

A calm feeling of the most perfect tranquility succeeded the most tumultuous sensation.... Nor was I in any bodily pain. On the contrary, my sensations were now of rather a pleasurable cast .... Though the senses were thus deadened, not so the mind; its activity seemed to be invigorated in a ratio which defies all description; for thought rose after thought with a rapidity of succession that is not only indescribable, but probably inconceivable, by anyone who has been himself in a similar situation. The course of these thoughts I can even now in a great measure retrace: the event that had just taken place .... Thus, traveling backwards, every incident of my past life seemed to me to glance across my recollection in retrograde procession ... the whole period of my existence seemed to be placed before me in a kind of panoramic view. (The Undiscovered Country section, para. 4)

Throughout history and in different cultures, NDEs have been a part of human experiences. They appear in old writings and recent stories, showing us how life is fragile and hinting at unknown mysteries beyond our understanding.

Incredible Stories of Near-Death Experiences

Rob's Family Reunion

Picture Rob Blackmore, a man of quiet resolve, driving home to his small town in Maine after a long day's work. The familiar stretch of road unfolded before him, a ribbon of asphalt winding through the landscape as dusk painted the sky in hues of gold and lavender.

In the tranquility of that moment, fate intervened in the form of a sudden collision with an oncoming vehicle. The impact was jarring, as the world around him faded into darkness and consciousness slipped away. First responders arrived on the scene, but their efforts to revive him proved futile. Rob was declared lifeless.

Yet, as his physical body lay motionless, Rob's spirit started on a journey beyond the confines of mortal existence. In the hush of that ethereal realm, he found himself standing on the threshold of something extraordinary—his very own glimpse of Heaven.

Imagine the sensation of lightness—of being cradled in a love so profound it defies description. For Rob, this was not a dream but a reality more vivid than anything he had ever known. Surrounding him were those he had loved and lost; their presence was a calm to his soul.

Before him stood the gates of Heaven, their beauty transcendent and awe-inspiring. Each step toward them was a testament to the boundless wonder awaiting him. He wondered what mysteries lay beyond? What revelations awaited his heart?

In that moment, Rob's journey became more than a mere passage from one existence to the next—it was a revelation of the divine. As he crossed the threshold into the unknown, he was met with a profound sense of peace and a large group of loved ones who had passed.

They wrapped him in love but asked him the question: "What of those he left behind, whose hearts now bore the burden of grief and longing?" He was given a choice in that moment, and assured they would be there waiting for him when it was truly his time.

Art's Journey to Heaven

Art, a pastor, believes his journey is a testament to the enduring mysteries of Heaven and it began with a diagnosis that shattered the illusion of invincibility. At 54, faced with the harsh reality of a terminal lung disease, Art found himself thrust into a tumultuous odyssey of illness and introspection.

The turning point came within the sterile confines of an operating theater, where Art lay suspended between life and death. As the surgeons toiled to restore his failing lungs, an unexpected transition occurred. Suddenly liberated from the constraints of his physical form, Art found himself enveloped in a realm beyond mortal comprehension.

In that transcendent moment, Art was transported to a place of blinding light, where the burdens of pain and suffering dissolved into oblivion. Within the celestial splendor, he was granted a glimpse into the indescribable beauty of Heaven itself: a realm of pure serenity and divine grace.

Yet, even amid the celestial splendor, Art's thoughts turned to the earthly realm and the selfless act of generosity that made his journey possible. In a poignant encounter, he found himself face-to-face with the soul of his donor, a silent witness to the transformative power of compassion and altruism.

With gratitude in his heart, Art offered thanks to the unknown benefactor as a gesture of reverence for the gift of life bestowed upon him. And as swiftly as he had departed, he found himself once more tethered to the mortal world—a vessel of grace and gratitude in the wake of divine intervention.

The road to recovery was arduous, fraught with challenges and setbacks, yet guided by the unseen hand of providence. In the wake of his near-death experience, Art found comfort in the knowledge that he was never truly alone and that angels walked beside him in moments of despair and doubt.

Today, as he stands on the threshold of a new dawn, Art is filled with a profound sense of purpose and gratitude. For, in the wake of adversity, he has found redemption—a renewed faith in the boundless love that transcends the barriers of mortality.

And though the mysteries of Heaven remain shrouded in enigma, Art takes comfort in the knowledge that something unimaginably powerful is ever-present; there's hope in the darkest of nights.

Charles's Dentures

Charles found himself in a deep coma, his consciousness traversing realms beyond the tangible.

As he lay there, he met a caring nurse who was a source of comfort and kindness during his journey. When he came back to consciousness, he amazed her with words that went beyond the physical realm. He talked about recognizing her, even in the midst of the chaos of trying to revive him months earlier. What he said next touched everyone deeply.

With clarity born of an otherworldly knowing, he described the precise location of his dentures, a seemingly mundane detail within the gravity of his condition. He spoke of the cart where she had placed them, every detail rendered with a clarity that defied explanation. And lo and behold, when she ventured to verify his words, she found his dentures exactly where he had described, a testament to the inexplicable mysteries that intertwine our lives with the realms beyond.

Sandra's Heart Attack

It was like any other Monday night. She had showered, prepped the coffee pot for the following morning and fed the cat. She read two chapters in her book and drifted off to sleep. Two short hours later, Sandra would be startled awake by body tremors and a stabbing pain in her chest. She scrambled to wake her husband, he called 911, and that was the last thing she remembered.

She recalls being shocked and becoming alert once in the ambulance, and the next "memory" she has is a conversation with her sister, who died five years earlier. Clear as day, her sister was using a stern voice and telling her to fight. "You can do this; it is not time for you to be here yet."

Sandra recalls gasping awake, opening her eyes to see a nurse, and reaching for her arm. "Please do not let me die."

It would be three weeks later that Sandra would confide in her husband about this meeting she had with her sister. As tears streamed down her face, she admitted to feeling exhausted and wanting to give up for a brief moment. It was then her sister showed up. She tells everyone just how mad her sister was. Yes, she felt loved, Yes, she felt light and warm, but it was evident that she was not yet welcome.

She thanks both her sister and the health care team for keeping her alive and well.

***

As we conclude this chapter on NDEs, I hope you've found comfort in the profound stories shared within these pages. These accounts, often shrouded in mystery and wonder, offer glimpses into realms beyond our earthly existence. They remind us that there is so much more to life than what meets the eye.

Perhaps you've been touched by the tale of someone who journeyed to the brink of death and returned with a newfound sense of peace and purpose. Or maybe you've found comfort in the idea that our loved ones who have passed on are not truly gone, but simply waiting for us on the other side.

We are all travelers on this journey called life, and we each carry within us the spark of divinity. Even during our most challenging times, there is brightness. Even within our profound sorrow, there is optimism.

As we move forward into the next chapter, let us take a moment to reflect on the mysteries of Heaven and the purpose of our existence. Let us ponder the meaning of our lives and the legacy we wish to leave behind. And above all, let us hold onto the belief that love endures, transcending time and space to unite us with those we cherish most.

In the pages ahead, we will delve into the nature of Heaven, and look at the profound connection between our earthly existence and the spiritual realm.

CHAPTER 7:

What If There Is No Heaven?

As we journey together through the mysteries of Heaven, I understand that not everyone shares the same beliefs about what lies beyond this earthly existence. Some among us may grapple with the notion that there might not be a Heaven at all. You may find yourself in this contemplative space, questioning the existence of an afterlife. In fact, your inquiry is a profound and courageous exploration into the depths of human understanding and spirituality.

In this chapter, we take a thoughtful jaunt down a path questioning what it would mean if there was no Heaven or afterlife. This topic makes us question our beliefs about life and death, forcing us to face our own mortality and the purpose of our lives.

For some, the absence of Heaven may evoke feelings of uncertainty and, perhaps, even fear or sadness. After all, the promise of an eternal paradise has long served as a source of comfort and peace for countless souls throughout history. But what if we were to consider an alternative perspective? What if, in the absence of Heaven, we discover a different kind of beauty and purpose in our lives?

As we move further into this topic, my intention is not to persuade or convince you of any particular viewpoint. Instead, I invite you to join me in a spirit of open-minded exploration and introspection. Together, let us ponder the implications of a world without Heaven, and in doing so, uncover new insights and revelations about the nature of our human experience.

Regardless of where your beliefs ultimately lead you, my hope is that this chapter serves as a sanctuary for contemplation, a safe space for grappling with complex questions, and a place of hope amid uncertainty. Remember that the journey itself is often as enlightening as the destination, and in our shared quest for understanding we find strength, resilience, and a deeper appreciation for the mysteries that bind us all.

Respecting Differences

It's crucial to acknowledge and respect the vast array of beliefs that people hold dear. In our diverse world, there are, indeed, religions and cultures that don't embrace the concept of

Heaven or any similar afterlife notion. And you know what? That's perfectly okay.

Some belief systems, like certain branches of Buddhism, focus more on the present moment and the cycle of reincarnation rather than a traditional heavenly realm. Others, like certain schools of thought in atheism or agnosticism, may not subscribe to the idea of an afterlife altogether, instead emphasizing the importance of living a meaningful life in the here and now.

These differences in belief aren't a cause for division or judgment, but rather an opportunity for us to expand our understanding and compassion. Just because someone's beliefs about the afterlife differ from ours doesn't make them any less valid or worthy of respect.

In fact, embracing diversity of belief can enrich our own spiritual journey. It challenges us to question our assumptions, deepen our empathy, and perhaps even find common ground with others despite our differences.

I recently came across an interesting study. One out of every four Americans do not believe in Heaven or Hell. It states that 7% believe in "a sort of afterlife," and 17% have a belief there is no afterlife. I charted the results below (Weber, 2021; Pew Research Center, 2021):

Breakdown	Heaven	Hell
All U.S. Adults	73%	62%
Men	68%	59%
Women	78%	65%

Breakdown	Heaven	Hell
Ages 18-49	67%	58%
Ages 50+	80%	67%
Catholic	90%	74%
Protestant	93%	84%
Evangelical	96%	91%
Unaffiliated	37%	28%

I believe these statistics reveal that most American adults, no matter their religion or background, seek comfort. They all yearn for peace and eternal happiness, showing how humans naturally want to believe in something bigger and more meaningful than everyday life. Is that Heaven? That is a personal choice. We do know it is a place of happiness and calm.

It is evident that men and women of all ages ponder these deep questions in their own ways. However, a shared desire for something beyond the physical world unites them all.

For the younger population, Heaven and Hell can be like a guiding light. But for older people, thoughts about the afterlife provide comfort as they face the end of life.

So, what do we know for sure? We are as unique as fingerprints, and each of us as distinct as snowflakes. Therefore, it's no surprise that our belief in Heaven would be just as individual and varied.

We understand that not everyone believes in an afterlife in Heaven. This is an important part of the complex and unique human experience.

For some people, not believing in Heaven doesn't make life empty. Instead, it helps them focus on enjoying the present moments, finding happiness and purpose in this life rather than hoping for rewards in the afterlife.

Some believe that if this life is all there is, then every experience, every connection, and every moment becomes all the more precious. It's like realizing that the fleeting beauty of a sunset or the warmth of a loved one's embrace is not just a prelude to something greater but is the very essence of what it means to be alive.

Without the belief in Heaven, we're challenged to find meaning in the everyday moments, in the kindness we show to others, in the pursuit of knowledge and understanding, and in the love we share with friends and family. It's a different way of looking at things but one that can be just as profound and enriching.

So, whether you believe in Heaven or not, it's important to honor and respect each other's perspectives. Let's recognize that we're all on this journey together—seeking understanding, connection, and meaning in our own unique ways. And in doing so, let's find common ground, compassion, and hope.

Happiness and a Belief in Heaven

You know, life has this funny way of weaving together happiness and the mysteries of what comes next—like a dance between the known and the unknown. And lately, there's been some chatter about how our beliefs about Heaven and Hell might sway the scales of happiness in our lives. Let's unpack that together.

There's this fascinating study out there—done by the University of Oregon and Simon Fraser University. They explored the beliefs people hold about Heaven and Hell, using data from all around the world. What they found was intriguing: It seems that believing in Heaven tends to nudge people toward a sunnier disposition. It's like having that extra spring in your step, knowing there's something beautiful waiting beyond the horizon (Shariff & Aknin, 2014).

In the study they talked to a diverse group of Americans. They talked to a diverse mix of people from different walks of life and beliefs. And what they found echoed the global pattern:

Those who leaned toward beliefs about Heaven tended to report higher levels of happiness and contentment. Meanwhile, what about those who gave a bit more thought to Hell? Well, they weren't feeling quite as rosy (Shariff & Aknin, 2014).

But hey, it's not just about what we believe; it's also about how those beliefs make us feel. The study showed that whether we're thinking about Heaven or Hell can really sway our emotional landscape. It's like our beliefs have this power to color the world around us, painting it with shades of joy or shadows of despair.

So, what's the takeaway from all this? Well, it's a reminder that our beliefs aren't just abstract ideas; they're woven into our daily lives. And, yes, a belief in Heaven can offer a glimmer of hope and happiness into our lives.

As we ponder the complexities of belief and happiness, let's remember that we're all on this journey together—exploring, questioning, and discovering the wonders that lie beyond the horizon. And in that shared pilgrimage, may we find not just answers but a deeper sense of connection, purpose, and joy.

The Impact of Not Believing

Let's explore together the impact of not believing in Heaven. The idea of Heaven is significant in shaping our views on life, death, and the meaning of existence, regardless of our religious or cultural background.

Imagine a world where the notion of Heaven fades into obscurity—where the belief in an afterlife dissipates like mist in the morning sun. It can be a sobering thought, right? For many, the belief in Heaven serves as a comforting reassurance that there's something beyond this earthly realm, something eternal and transcendent.

On a societal level, when people no longer believe in Heaven, it can cause a significant change in the values and attitudes of the community. Our shared understanding of what is right and wrong, our reasons for existence, and the significance we find in life are often influenced by religious and spiritual beliefs, many of which involve the idea of an afterlife in paradise. If this belief in Heaven is absent, society may experience a major shift, where moral questions and the purpose of life are either not addressed or are redefined within a non-religious framework.

Culturally, the impact would be far-reaching. Throughout history, depictions of Heaven have inspired art, literature, music, and countless other forms of creative expression. The absence of belief in Heaven could diminish the richness of cultural heritage, leaving behind a void where once there was wonder and awe.

Religiously, the implications are profound. For billions around the world, the belief in Heaven is a central tenet of their faith, providing comfort in times of grief and guiding principles for living a virtuous life. Without this belief, religious institutions may struggle to maintain relevance, and people may grapple with a sense of spiritual emptiness or disillusionment.

It's important to remember that people have different beliefs and values. Not everyone follows the same religion or culture, so the idea of Heaven doesn't affect everyone in the same way. Some people find it freeing not to believe in Heaven, which can lead them to think more about life's big questions and focus on the present moment.

Ultimately, whether one believes in Heaven or not, the human experience is imbued with a profound sense of mystery and wonder. Our beliefs shape our perceptions of reality, but they do not define the essence of our existence. In the absence of certainty, we are invited to embrace the beauty of uncertainty, to find comfort in the interconnectedness of all things, and to cherish the precious moments we have in this fleeting, wondrous journey called life.

Losing Faith After a Loved One Dies

Losing someone dear to us can shatter our world in ways we never imagined. It's like the ground beneath our feet suddenly gives way, leaving us suspended in a void of grief and confusion. I know this journey all too well, and if you're reading this, chances are you're grappling with similar emotions.

When we lose a loved one, it's not just their physical presence that we mourn. We mourn the future we envisioned with them, the conversations we'll never have, and the moments we'll never share. It's a profound loss that pierces through the very fabric of our being, leaving us raw and vulnerable.

In the midst of such intense pain, it's natural for our faith to waver. We may find ourselves questioning everything we once held dear. The beliefs that once provided comfort may now seem like distant echoes in the darkness of our despair.

Feelings of disbelief, anger, and confusion are like turbulent waves crashing against the shores of our soul. We may wonder why this had to happen, why our prayers seemed to go unanswered, and why a higher power would allow such suffering to exist.

I want you to know that it's okay to question. It's okay to be angry, to feel lost, and to doubt. Grief is a messy, unpredictable mountain of emotions. And within it, it's natural to re-evaluate our beliefs about life, death, and the afterlife.

The concept of an afterlife, once a source of comfort, may now seem like a distant dream. We may struggle to reconcile the idea of a loving, just universe with the harsh reality of loss and pain. The very foundations of our faith may feel shaky, as if the ground beneath us is crumbling away.

Within the darkness, there is hope. It's often in our moments of deepest despair that we find the strength to rise again. It's in our moments of questioning that we discover a deeper, more authentic faith—one that can withstand the storms of doubt and uncertainty.

Perhaps the afterlife isn't meant to be understood with our rational minds but, instead, felt with our hearts. Maybe it's not about having all the answers but embracing the mystery of what lies beyond. And perhaps, just maybe, our loved ones are not truly gone but simply exist in a different form, watching over us with love and guidance.

So if you're struggling with doubts and fears, know that this is normal. Reach out to others who have walked this path before you. Find comfort in the beauty of nature, the warmth of human connection, and the quiet whispers of your own soul.

And above all, hold onto hope. For even in the darkest of nights, there are stars shining brightly above, reminding us that light always follows darkness and love always triumphs over loss.

Personal Stories of Lost Faith

Jason and His Mom

Several months ago, Jason's beloved mother passed away suddenly, shattering his world. Their deep connection made coping with life without her seem impossible.

Throughout his life, Jason had strong faith in the Lord, managing tough times and treasuring moments of grace. But since his mother passed away, his faith has been deeply shaken.

Now, he struggles to find the words to pray, except to ask for mercy for his mother and strength for himself as he mourns, because everything he once held dear feels like it's slipping away.

Though he still holds onto some of his beliefs, the pain of questions and doubts burdens his heart heavily. Seeing others in similar grief and clinging to the hope of reuniting with their loved ones forever, while knowing not everyone will experience that promise, feels daunting.

Desperately, Jason searches for a renewed faith in the boundless mercy and compassion of God, even when logic and scripture seem to contradict. The notion of judgment after death is a heavy burden to bear, and he longs for a glimmer of hope that, perhaps, salvation is more inclusive than they've been led to believe.

Since the passing of his mother, he finds himself unable to pray, sing, or even read scripture. The shattered pieces of his faith seem irreparable.

Jason decided to have a conversation with a few people in his congregation, and they offered him some valuable advice. The first thing he did was acknowledge his faith was shaken, yet continue to engage in spiritual practices that resonate with him. These practices started to provide a sense of connection to something greater than himself and offer moments of comfort and reflection.

He realized he needed time. It wasn't his mother's passing that made him question his faith; it was his own beliefs. He had to determine what he believed had happened to his mother, would he reunite with her, and was she okay? Once he leaned into his faith and found comfort in his answers, he could move on.

Ellen and Her Dad

It was a hot and sunny day in August 1991. Ellen, then just 7 years old, recalls the events vividly. Her 33-year-old mother gathered her and her four siblings into the car, planning to bring lunch to their father, who was working in the fields. Life on their farm was idyllic, filled with outdoor adventures, visits to neighbors, and a strong sense of community.

As they embarked on their journey, fate intervened in the form of a flat tire. Undeterred, Ellen's mother began changing the tire, though her frustration at the delay was palpable. Suddenly, two cars approached from behind—it was Ellen's grandparents. Their solemn expressions signaled that something was terribly wrong. Ellen's mother, upon receiving the devastating news of her husband's passing, collapsed in anguish.

In the months that followed, the family faced immense challenges. They were forced to split up, seeking refuge in the homes of relatives while they navigated their grief. Eventually, they resettled in a new home in town, but adjusting to this new reality was arduous. Ellen's mother had to take on full-time work at the local grocery store—a stark departure from her previous role as a stay-at-home mom. The burden of managing the household fell heavily upon her shoulders, yet she remained steadfast in her devotion to her children and their faith.

Despite the upheaval, the family found comfort in their unwavering belief in God. Ellen, however, struggled to reconcile her faith with the tragedy that fell upon them. Watching her mother's anguish and witnessing their family's fragmentation left her questioning why God would allow such suffering.

Their church community rallied around them and offered support, guidance, and unwavering faith. From attending church camp to seeking counsel from Christian mentors, Ellen and her siblings found strength in the love and compassion of those around them.

Ellen believes it was through the support of their family, friends, and church community that she found the resilience to persevere, emerging from her grief with a deeper understanding of faith and a renewed sense of purpose.

Joshua and His Baby Daughter

Two days before Thanksgiving, Joshua went to wake up his 3-month-old baby girl from her nap and noticed she wasn't breathing. He asked his older daughter to call 911.

As he talked to the emergency operator on the phone, Joshua frantically tried to resuscitate his baby while calling on Jesus to help him.

An ambulance came some few minutes later, and his baby was rushed to the hospital with Joshua anxiously praying. A few hours later, his daughter was pronounced dead.

Joshua refused to believe she was gone. He and his wife prayed all night with a few people from church for his baby to wake up, but she did not. It would take days for both he and his wife to finally accept that his baby was gone.

He was completely heartbroken and devastated. Time stopped for him, and he felt like he was in this deep pit of hopelessness that he would never come out of. His family was in utter anguish.

All of Joshua's dreams of watching his daughter grow up were destroyed. Losing a child is a parent's worst nightmare, and

Joshua experienced the most excruciating pain of his life when it happened.

Joshua didn't cope very well. He became very angry, disappointed, and sad, and severe anxiety set in.

He was fully convinced that God had left him when he needed Him most. He could not understand why He permitted his daughter to die and why He refused to wake her up. He struggled to comprehend why God would take one of his children away? Why was he being punished?

His church family was very supportive. They stepped up and helped organize the baby's funeral, as Joshua and his wife just could not. Joshua felt so blessed to be supported by a loving church family. Unfortunately, he felt that some comments from friends and family minimized his loss. He did not find comments like, "Be grateful you have three other children," or, "She is an angel in Heaven forever watching over you," helpful.

Looking back on his journey, Joshua can say that he has grown, and he is still growing. The painful loss of his daughter opened him up to new relationships and new opportunities. It has made him a better listener and more empathetic.

Even when he was upset and mad at God in the beginning, he had no one else to turn to. He cried, screamed, and threw things, but God always comforted him. He realized that nothing can break his bond with God. Although he still has questions, he's okay with not having all the answers until he reaches Heaven.

***

As we conclude this chapter, perhaps you find yourself lingering on a question that echoes through the depths of your soul: What if there is no Heaven? It's a query that has crossed the minds of many, especially in moments of profound loss and uncertainty.

Let's pause to think about what a world would be like without the idea of Heaven. Picture a society where there is no belief in a divine realm, and the focus is on chasing material wealth and temporary joys. In this scenario, how do people hold onto hope during tough times? What do they rely on when faced with overwhelming sadness?

As we move forward into the next chapter, let's welcome the endless opportunities ahead. Regardless of our beliefs about life after death, exploring our role in the universe invites us to open our hearts and minds. This journey encourages us to delve into our humanity, fostering kindness and understanding toward ourselves and those around us.

CHAPTER 8:

What If Heaven Is Real

...◈...

Recent studies shed light on the powerful influence that beliefs about Heaven can have on our lives (Fitouchi & Singh, 2022). It's fascinating to consider how these narratives, deeply rooted in various cultures, shape not only our thoughts but also our behaviors. Psychologist Manvir Singh highlights that our inclination toward these supernatural beliefs isn't merely a matter of blind faith but, rather, a cognitive inclination deeply embedded within us (Travers, 2022).

But let's step back for a moment. What if Heaven is real? What if beyond the place we live lies a realm of unimaginable beauty and peace? The idea of this possibility can deeply move us, going beyond logic to encourage us to explore unknown realms.

In times of grief, the concept of Heaven often emerges as a sign of hope—a comforting thought that death is not forever. We hope that when our time comes, we will be greeted by those who have passed and welcomed into this amazing, warm, and beautiful place.

In the chapter ahead, we will talk more about what life looks like when we do believe in Heaven. Do we live our lives differently? Are we always morally aligning ourselves with intent to reunite with those we have lost? Let's dive in.

A Belief in Heaven

Heaven is very important to many people because it gives them comfort, hope, and a feeling of purpose. Believing in Heaven can make people feel better during sad times because they think there is a peaceful and happy place where they can be with their loved ones forever.

The idea of Heaven gives hope by promising fair and rewarding results for our actions in life. It assures us that justice will win, and any suffering now will be fixed later. This hope motivates us to keep going, find purpose in challenges, and live morally.

Believing in Heaven can give life a purpose by seeing it as a journey towards a higher goal. It helps people live better by focusing on values like compassion and kindness. The idea of Heaven inspires individuals to lead meaningful lives, grow spiritually, and help others.

The importance of whether or not Heaven is real varies based on a person's beliefs. For those with religious or spiritual beliefs that mention Heaven, its existence is very meaningful. It brings peace and hope in some of our darkest times. When we are in the throes of grief, we cling to a belief that our loved ones are in a beautiful and safe place, waiting to see us again. Heaven gives believers a sense of purpose, granting us a reward of eternal happiness in the afterlife. Having a belief in Heaven can also impact our moral values and how people behave toward others. If we choose to believe that doing good here on Earth grants us access to the same Heaven where our loved ones are, we may choose to do better.

So Many Questions

The one certainty that is inescapable is the amount of questions we will come up against when discussing beliefs in Heaven. Especially when we lose someone we love, those questions begin to surface and we are desperate to find the answers.

Here's a list of questions that people may ponder when contemplating the existence of Heaven:

1. Is Heaven a real place or just a concept?

2. What evidence supports the existence of Heaven?

3. Do different religions have different interpretations of Heaven?

4. What does Heaven look like?

5. Can near-death experiences provide insights into the existence of Heaven?

6. How does the concept of Heaven align with scientific understanding of the universe?

7. If Heaven exists, is it a physical place or a state of being?

8. Do animals go to Heaven?

9. Are there levels or stages of Heaven?

10. Can we communicate with loved ones in Heaven?

11. Do our actions on Earth affect our admission to Heaven?

12. How does the concept of Heaven relate to concepts of justice and fairness?

13. If there is a Heaven, what purpose does it serve?

14. Can people of different faiths coexist in Heaven?

15. How does the concept of Heaven impact the way we live our lives on Earth?

These questions reflect the diverse range of thoughts and considerations that people may have when grappling with the notion of Heaven or grief. Each question offers an opportunity for reflection, exploration, and deeper understanding of this profound and timeless concept. Let's try to answer as many as we can. Any that I skip over have been thoroughly discussed in previous chapters.

Is Heaven a Real Place or Just a Concept?

While the answer ultimately depends on one's perspective and faith, let's explore both angles.

From a religious or spiritual standpoint, many people firmly believe that Heaven is, indeed, a real place—an eternal realm beyond the physical confines of our world. As we've discussed, many various religious traditions and descriptions of Heaven abound, ranging from serene gardens to celestial cities; each one offers a vision of unparalleled beauty, peace, and joy. For believers, Heaven represents the ultimate reward for a life lived in accordance with divine principles—a place of reunion with loved ones, spiritual growth, and eternal bliss.

However, some people see Heaven more as a symbolic idea representing hope, comfort, and something beyond our earthly lives. They view Heaven as a metaphor for our deepest desires: a perfect place that goes beyond what we experience on Earth. While not completely dismissing the idea of an afterlife, supporters of this view often highlight the symbolic and allegorical meanings of heavenly symbols, placing greater importance on their psychological and existential implications.

What Evidence Supports the Existence of Heaven?

While there may not be empirical scientific evidence in the traditional sense, believers often draw upon a variety of sources to affirm their conviction in Heaven's reality. Here are some considerations:

- **Religious texts and traditions:** For many, religious scriptures and traditions provide foundational evidence of Heaven's existence. Texts such as the Bible, the Qur'an, the Vedas, and others contain descriptions of Heaven and the afterlife, offering believers guidance, comfort, and assurance in the reality of these realms.

- **Near-death experiences (NDEs):** As discussed in Chapter 6, accounts of NDEs—where people report profound visions and sensations during periods of clinical death—are often cited as evidence of an afterlife. While these experiences vary widely and can be interpreted in different ways, many find them compelling evidence of the existence of a heavenly realm beyond our physical world.

- **Spiritual experiences:** Personal experiences of feeling close to God, moments of deep connection, and spiritual insights can strongly convince people that Heaven is real. These experiences—whether during prayer, meditation, or other spiritual activities—help believers feel directly connected to the spiritual and strengthen their belief in Heavenly realms.

- **Personal testimonies:** Testimonies of those who claim to have encountered Heaven—whether through visions, dreams, or mystical experiences—can be compelling evidence for believers. While subjective in nature, these accounts often carry profound emotional resonance and serve as powerful affirmations of faith.

What Does Heaven Look Like?

Descriptions of Heaven vary widely across different religious and spiritual traditions; even within individual beliefs, Heaven can be envisioned in many unique ways. While specific depictions may differ, there are common themes that often emerge in descriptions of Heaven:

- **Celestial beauty:** Many descriptions of Heaven emphasize its incomparable beauty and splendor. It's often portrayed as a place of breathtaking landscapes, serene gardens, and radiant light—an environment of unparalleled perfection and harmony.

- **Eternal peace and joy:** Heaven is commonly described as a realm of eternal peace, where suffering and sorrow are replaced by unending joy and happiness.

It's envisioned as a sanctuary free from pain, conflict, and the trials of earthly life.

- **Divine presence:** Across religious traditions, Heaven is associated with the presence of the holy: the ultimate source of love, wisdom, and compassion. It's a place where believers are united with the sacred in a profound and intimate union, experiencing the fullness of holy grace and presence.

- **Reunion with loved ones:** Many visions of Heaven include the idea of reunion with departed loved ones— a joyous gathering of souls where relationships are restored and bonds are strengthened for eternity.

- **Spiritual growth and enlightenment:** Heaven is often portrayed as a realm of spiritual growth and enlightenment, where souls continue to evolve and progress in their journey toward spiritual perfection. It's a place of learning, exploration, and transformation, where people strive for greater wisdom and understanding.

- **Eternal life:** In many beliefs, Heaven is synonymous with eternal life: a state of existence that transcends the limitations of time and mortality. It's a realm where the soul lives on in perpetuity, free from the constraints of earthly existence.

- **Individualized experience:** While there are common themes in descriptions of Heaven, many believe that each person's experience of Heaven is unique and tailored to their own spiritual journey and aspirations. It's a deeply personal and intimate encounter with the divine, reflecting the individual's deepest desires and goals.

Descriptions of Heaven may vary, but they all share a message of hope, going beyond earthly understanding. Whether seen as a real place or a symbol of spiritual truths, Heaven encourages believers to think about life's mysteries, and the endless love and grace of the holy.

How Does the Concept of Heaven Align With Scientific Understanding of the Universe?

The concept of Heaven, deeply rooted in religious and spiritual traditions, often raises questions about its compatibility with scientific understanding of the universe. While science primarily deals with empirical observations and natural phenomena, and Heaven is often considered a transcendent realm beyond the physical world, there are ways in which these two perspectives can be reconciled:

- **Metaphorical interpretation:** Some people and theologians see Heaven as a symbol of spiritual truths rather than a real place. They view it as representing states of consciousness, spiritual enlightenment, or moral ideals—which connects with scientific studies on human psychology, morality, and consciousness.

- **Epistemological distinction:** Science and religion operate within different domains of knowledge; science seeks to understand the natural world through empirical observation and experimentation, while religion addresses questions of meaning, purpose, and transcendence. Recognizing the distinct methodologies and goals of each discipline allows for a respectful coexistence between scientific inquiry and religious belief.

- **Personal beliefs and interpretations:** Many hold both scientific and religious beliefs, viewing them as complementary rather than conflicting perspectives. For these people, scientific understanding of the universe provides insights into the workings of the natural world, while religious beliefs offer a framework for grappling with existential questions and finding meaning and purpose in life.

- **Openness to mystery:** Both science and religion acknowledge the limits of human knowledge and understanding. While science seeks to uncover the mechanisms underlying natural phenomena, it acknowledges that there may be mysteries beyond its current scope. Similarly, religious traditions often emphasize the mystery of the celestial and the ineffable nature of spiritual realities, inviting believers to embrace humility and wonder in the face of the unknown.

- **Interdisciplinary dialogue:** Increasingly, there is recognition of the value of interdisciplinary dialogue between science and religion. Scholars in fields such as theology, philosophy, and psychology engage in conversations with scientists to explore questions at the intersection of these disciplines, fostering mutual understanding and enriching both scientific and religious inquiry.

Ultimately, although Heaven may not align perfectly with scientific explanations, we can still explore and understand it by considering it alongside scientific knowledge of the universe. By staying open-minded, curious, and willing to discuss across different fields, we can enhance our comprehension of both nature and the spiritual aspects of life.

Do Animals Go to Heaven?

The question of whether animals go to Heaven is one that has sparked contemplation, debate, and curiosity among people of various religious and spiritual beliefs. While there is no definitive answer, as interpretations vary across different traditions and people, let's explore some perspectives on this intriguing question:

- **Religious teachings:** In some religions, it's not clear if animals have an afterlife. But some people believe that animals, like all living beings, might have a place in celestial plans for eternal life.

- **Concepts of justice and compassion:** Some people believe that animals can go to Heaven because they see them as feeling beings capable of love and suffering. They think a fair and loving God would save all creatures, no matter what species they are.

- **Personal beliefs and interpretations:** Many people believe that the connection between humans and animals is so special that it can go beyond death, leading to the idea of reuniting in a spiritual world based on personal experiences, spiritual insights, and moral beliefs.

- **Symbolic interpretations:** In certain religious and spiritual beliefs, animals symbolize divine qualities or spiritual truths. Although they don't have individual souls like humans, they are considered part of the interconnected web of life and appreciated for their value and contributions to nature.

- **Unknown mysteries:** The question of whether animals go to the afterlife is a mystery beyond our full understanding. We can think about it and look for answers, but we should remember our limits and respect the unknown.

Can We Communicate With Loved Ones in Heaven?

The idea of talking to our loved ones in Heaven is important to many people, especially those who have lost someone special. The answer to this question can be different based on what each person believes. Let's think about this question together:

- **Spiritual beliefs:** In certain religious and spiritual beliefs, followers think they can communicate with loved ones who have passed away through prayer, meditation, or spiritual activities. They believe that the connection between the living and the dead lasts even after physical death, enabling ongoing communication on a spiritual level.

- **Personal experiences:** Many people believe they receive messages from deceased loved ones through dreams, visions, or meaningful signs. These experiences, though personal and open to interpretation, can bring comfort to those mourning a loss.

- **Mediumship and spiritualism:** Some people seek out mediums or spiritual practitioners to communicate with loved ones who have passed away. Mediums say they can connect with spirits and pass on messages from them, providing comfort and closure to those who want to reach out to their departed family and friends.

- **Symbolic interpretations:** Even if someone doesn't believe in talking to those who have passed, memories of loved ones can still deeply affect them. They might feel better by doing rituals, following traditions, and remembering moments that help them feel their loved ones are still with them.

- **Unanswered questions:** Communication with loved ones who have passed away is a concept that goes beyond what we can fully grasp. Some people may feel comfort in thinking it's possible, while others struggle with not knowing for sure, recognizing that we can't know everything and that the afterlife is complex.

Whether we can talk to loved ones in Heaven is a personal conviction. Some find comfort in believing they can communicate with those who have passed away. Others find peace in memories and the lasting impact of the departed. Regardless of beliefs, the love and connection with lost loved ones shape and enrich the lives of those still here, providing strength, inspiration, and eternal memories.

How Does the Concept of Heaven Relate to Concepts of Justice and Fairness?

The concept of Heaven and its relationship to justice and fairness is a thought-provoking topic that invites contemplation on the nature of morality, accountability, and sacred judgment. Here are some perspectives on how these concepts intersect:

- **Divine justice:** In various religions, Heaven is portrayed as a place where holy justice prevails. It is seen as a reward for good deeds and moral behavior, and a place where wrongdoers face consequences for their actions. Essentially, Heaven symbolizes the idea of fairness, where good is rewarded and evil is punished.

- **Reward and punishment:** The concept of Heaven as a prize for good deeds and a consequence for bad behavior highlights the significance of being ethical and accountable in various religious teachings. People who believe in this idea may feel reassured that their actions in this life will have everlasting effects, with Heaven being the ultimate prize for living a life guided by holy values.

- **Equality and fairness:** The idea of Heaven makes people wonder about fairness in how holy rewards are given. People believe that in Heaven, everyone is equal in the eyes of the celestial, no matter their wealth, status, or power on Earth. Heaven is seen as a place where all souls are accepted and valued for their pure hearts and sincere intentions.

- **Redemption and mercy:** Many religions focus on celestial justice, redemption, and mercy. They teach that Heaven is not just for perfect people but also for those who admit their mistakes, seek forgiveness, and change for the better. This idea shows how grace and mercy can transform individuals, giving them a chance for redemption and spiritual growth.

- **Theodicy:** The connection between Heaven, justice, and fairness raises questions about why there is evil and suffering in the world. People who believe in Heaven struggle to understand how there can be injustice and pain on earth, looking for answers that bring comfort and purpose in difficult times.

Heaven is seen as a symbol of fairness, kindness, and something beyond this world. It gives believers hope, comfort, and guidance in dealing with life's challenges and questions. People think of it as a reward for being good, a sign of love for everyone, or a light in tough times—making us think about justice, fairness, and what happens to us after we die.

If There Is a Heaven, What Purpose Does It Serve?

The concept of Heaven serves multifaceted purposes across various religious and spiritual traditions, offering believers a source of hope, comfort, and meaning in the face of life's uncertainties. Here are some key purposes that Heaven is believed to serve:

- **Ultimate reward:** Many believers view Heaven as the ultimate reward for a life lived in accordance with divine principles and moral virtues. It is envisioned as a place of eternal bliss, where the righteous are granted entry to experience the fullness of sacred love, joy, and fulfillment. The promise of Heaven serves as a powerful incentive for believers to strive for goodness and righteousness in their earthly lives.

- **Eternal reunion:** Heaven is shown as a place where people who have passed away meet their family, friends, and ancestors. People who believe in this find comfort in the idea that death is not the end, but a move to a better place where relationships are renewed forever. The thought of reuniting with loved ones in Heaven brings peace and hope to those mourning the loss of a loved one.

- **Spiritual growth and fulfillment:** Heaven is like a school for the soul, where it learns and grows spiritually toward becoming spiritually whole. People think of Heaven as a place where the soul keeps learning and discovering new things, getting closer to understanding life's mysteries.

- **Transcendence of suffering:** Heaven is seen as a peaceful place without the difficulties of life on earth. It's a place of happiness and calmness where there is no more suffering or sadness. People believe that in Heaven, all pain and struggles are gone, and the soul can rest forever without mortal challenges.

- **Fulfillment of divine purpose:** For many believers, Heaven is where God's ultimate plan is fulfilled, and His love and power are fully present. It's a place where love, justice, and redemption come together perfectly, showing God's complete love and care over everything.

Can People of Different Faiths Coexist in Heaven?

This topic has led to thinking and discussions among theologians, scholars, and believers of various religions.

Although opinions on this vary, here are some things to think about:

- **Inclusivity and universality:** Many religious traditions emphasize the inclusivity and universality of divine love and salvation, suggesting that Heaven is accessible to all sincere seekers of truth, goodness, and spiritual fulfillment, regardless of their religious affiliation. Believers may find comfort in the belief that God's mercy transcends religious boundaries and welcomes all who earnestly seek holy grace and redemption.

- **Interfaith dialogue and understanding:** In a world where people are more connected than ever, many now see how important it is for different religions to talk and understand each other. This helps to build respect, cooperation, and peaceful living among individuals from various religious beliefs. Some religious experts support the idea of Heaven being open to different ways of reaching spiritual fulfillment and being saved.

- **Variability of beliefs:** Beliefs about Heaven and who can go there differ among religions. Some believe only followers of their faith can be saved, while others think people from different religions can also achieve salvation and spiritual fulfillment.

- **Personal convictions and interpretations:** Ultimately, beliefs about who can enter Heaven and how they can do so are very personal and can differ greatly, even among people in the same religion. Some people strongly believe in specific rules from their religious texts—while others focus on love, compassion, and empathy as important values that go beyond religious boundaries.

- **Mystery and transcendence:** The question of who can co-exist in Heaven ultimately touches on profound mysteries that transcend human understanding. Believers grapple with questions about the nature of celestial justice, the significance of religious diversity, and the ultimate destiny of the human soul— recognizing the limits of human knowledge and the vastness of divine grace.

In the end, the question of whether people from different faiths can live together in Heaven requires humility, compassion, and a readiness to talk and think about different religions. Even though beliefs may vary, followers of various faiths unite in their desire for love, peace, and spiritual satisfaction—which go beyond the things that set them apart.

As we conclude this chapter contemplating the possibility of Heaven, I hope you're feeling a sense of peace settling within you, like a gentle breeze soothing the soul. The mysteries we've explored together have undoubtedly stirred emotions, sparked questions, and, perhaps, even offered glimpses of hope in the midst of uncertainty. And now, as we move into the final chapter, I want to invite you to embrace the excitement that comes with discovery and understanding.

What if there is a Heaven? What if beyond this earthly realm lies a place of unimaginable beauty, where love reigns supreme and every tear is wiped away? It's a question that has echoed through the corridors of human hearts since time immemorial. And though we may never have all the answers in this lifetime, our exploration has lit pathways of possibility, avenues of belief, and reservoirs of faith.

But Heaven is more than just thinking and imagining. It's in our hearts, in the hope that never dies, and in the love that unites us all. It's where everyone finds peace, dreams, and love.

In the final chapter, we will review all we have uncovered: scriptures, theologians' insights, near-death experiences' revelations, and Heavenly visions. Let's create a clear picture of understanding, a collection of insights, and a hopeful message. Get ready for the final leg of our journey together, where we celebrate the truths we've found and the lasting importance of faith, hope, and love.

CHAPTER 9:

A Summary of Beliefs and Moving Through Grief

...◈...

Throughout our time together, we've discussed grief, the afterlife, the concept of Heaven, and many challenging questions.

Like many, I found my life altered by deep loss. When I lost my father, it changed how I saw life and death. My strong beliefs didn't seem enough to explain my sadness or my desire to be close to him again. I felt lost between faith and doubt, looking for a deeper truth.

Many of us start thinking about Heaven and the afterlife when we face the reality of death. Whether this begins as we age or when we lose someone who we love, our beliefs can change a lot. What we were once sure about might now seem uncertain, filled with questions.

Many of us realize that Heaven is not just a place we go to after we die. It's a feeling we can experience in our daily lives: in memories of loved ones, shared laughter, and the love we leave behind.

Our loved ones who have passed away are not far away in a distant place. I choose to believe they are in the loving embrace of God, always with us, shaping our lives in ways we may not even realize.

When it comes to communicating with those who have passed away, there are many different ways to connect. Some feel comfort in signs and symbols, while others find a connection through prayer or intuition. What's important is the love that drives the communication, bringing together Heaven and Earth with strong bonds of affection.

Signs From Above

I Am Alive: My Dad and a Song

I was working in my home office on my third book, *Nature's Reach*. Writing about grief always stirs up emotions for me, bringing back memories of my dad's passing. I miss him dearly. That day, as I put pen to paper, I found myself in a creative flow. Words moved effortlessly and ideas sprang to mind. However, by mid-afternoon, I hit a roadblock. My train of thought derailed, leaving me consumed by thoughts of my dad.

I recalled the day when he passed. I was holding his hand as he took his last breath. It was horrible. Sitting at my desk, I broke down and called out to Dad, "I miss you. I hope wherever you are, you're okay. If you can give me a sign, I just need to know you're okay."

I sat there in silence and nothing happened. I wasn't surprised that nothing happened. Calling out to my dad and demanding a sign does not guarantee anything immediately. It's not as if my father is tethered to a cell phone and waiting on my text message.

I decided to take a break from writing and opened a web browser. I'm always curious, searching for cars and trucks, so I went to my favorite website. With over 40,000 trucks in the search results, I randomly picked one. I remember it was a Ford F150. It looked nice, so I clicked to view the 55 photos available.

What I saw next took my breath away. The photo that I was looking at was of the dashboard. I had a clear view of the steering wheel and instrument panel, and just to the right was the touchscreen, below which were the temperature controls. Displayed on the touchscreen was the radio station, 96.3, playing "I Am Alive" by The Parlotones.

This was my first time hearing of this group. I was in complete shock! Just 60 seconds earlier, I was calling out to my dad, asking for a sign that he was okay. A minute later, I'm looking at a photo with the words, "I Am Alive." Was this a coincidence? Possibly. But out of the 40,000 trucks, I picked that one and looked at those photos. I believe in my soul that this was a sign from my dad that he was alive in another realm and was okay.

I went straight to YouTube to hear the lyrics, even more convinced that it was a sign from my dad. The lyrics are incredible, discussing life and its meaning, and how my dad figured it out and believes in himself. A line from the song reads, "Myself, me, and I, we figured out life, figured that life is the eternal prize."

I sat there, unable to stop sobbing. I like to consider myself a rational person. I explore all possibilities and explanations. I knew this could be a coincidence, yes. But the chances of me asking my dad for a sign, and then moments later looking at a photo saying, "I Am Alive," must be a billion to one.

Courtney's Sign in the Clouds

Courtney and her brother shared a bond that was forged in the fires of siblinghood. Born a mere 16 months apart, they navigated life hand in hand, inseparable in their adventures. When he suffered a broken arm on the baseball field, she mirrored his injury on the soccer pitch. Their childhoods were a symphony of shared experiences, from losing teeth in synchrony to standing side by side at pivotal moments like her wedding, where he proudly served as her "best man."

Their lives continued to intertwine as they embarked on parenthood almost simultaneously. Courtney welcomed her daughter into the world, only for her brother to follow suit with the birth of his son 6 months later. Their familial ties seemed unbreakable, woven tightly together by love and shared memories.

However, life can be cruel in its unpredictability, and tragedy struck with devastating swiftness. At the young age of 31, Courtney's brother received a harrowing diagnosis: brain cancer. Despite a valiant fight, he was gone in a mere 5 months, leaving Courtney reeling in the wake of his absence. Her world shattered, forever altered by the void left in his passing.

In the days and months that followed, Courtney struggled to make sense of her grief. The pain was visceral, rendering simple tasks arduous and leaving her adrift in a sea of sorrow. In the stillness of the early morning, when darkness still clung to the world and the promise of dawn hung in the air, she would whisper to him, her voice a desperate plea for reassurance: "I need to know you are with me."

The thought of moving forward without him felt unfathomable—the notion of his absence unbearable. But in the depths of despair, a glimmer of hope emerged. A year and a month after his passing, as Courtney started on a road trip to celebrate her youngest sister's wedding, a celestial sign illuminated the path ahead. Gazing out the window, she was greeted by a sight that brought tears to her eyes: The clouds had formed the number 11, stark against the canvas of the sky.

For Courtney, the significance was profound. Eleven had always been her brother's number, a symbol of his presence in every facet of his life. From sports jerseys to tattoos, it was a constant reminder of his essence, with his spirit imprinted upon the very fabric of their shared history. And now, in this moment of serendipity, it served as a source of comfort and reassurance.

Since that fateful day, Courtney has found peace in the presence of 11, a silent reminder that her brother is never truly gone. In the mundane moments of daily life—from steamed bathroom mirrors to glowing phone screens—his spirit lingers as a silent guardian watching over her with unwavering love. And in the laughter of her daughter and the smile of her nephew, she finds echoes of his presence—a testament to the enduring power of sibling bonds and the eternal nature of love.

Lynn's Mom and Chipmunks

Lynn, a woman with a kind heart and precious memories, felt sad because her dear mother was no longer with her. She believed her mother's spirit lived on in the soft sounds of nature. In the sunny surroundings of Florida, Lynn remembered her mother's loving nature, which she showed not just to people but also to the animals at their old home.

Recalling how her mother used to feed chipmunks and squirrels at their old home, Lynn thought about it fondly. But now, in Florida, where chipmunks were not around, it reminded her of the distance from her childhood home.

Fate had a unique way of connecting things through time and space. Even though Lynn lived on the fourth floor of her condo, far from the busy woodland creatures, she was surprised to see a bold and curious squirrel looking through her glass door.

Week after week, the squirrel would show up, right on time, looking directly at Lynn with a strange sense of familiarity. During those brief moments of connection, Lynn sensed a stirring in her soul—a hint of her mother's essence intertwined with nature's beauty.

With every visit, Lynn felt comforted, knowing her mother's spirit was present and showing itself through the playful actions of a surprising visitor. She pictured her mother's laughter in the rustling leaves and her love in the gentle breeze.

And so, in the quietude of her sunlit sanctuary, Lynn embraced these encounters with open arms, knowing that—in the gaze of the squirrel—she glimpsed the essence of her mother's enduring love. Through the simple act of looking into her sliding glass door, the squirrel became a symbol of connection: a bridge between past and present, between the earthly realm and the one beyond.

Sweet Caroline: My Dad's Message in the Night

At the end of February 2020, I received a text message from my dad that was unlike any other. It would change me for the rest of my life. The message simply read, "Hey son, I just got the results back from my blood work. I have cancer and I'm riddled with it. There is nothing they can do. I will start chemo and radiation, but they can't stop it. Hey Ho. Love dad."

I couldn't believe what I was reading. I had so many questions; I couldn't believe that there was nothing that could be done. I texted my dad back and asked if we could FaceTime. He declined because he was too emotional. When my wife, Alison, got home from the office, I told her about the situation.

We started looking at flights to Liverpool, England. The Covid pandemic was just starting, but flight restrictions or masks were not yet an issue. I told my sister that we would be arriving in six days. She suggested we stay in a nearby hotel because my dad had not yet met my wife, and he may feel too emotional and need some privacy.

We booked a rental car and a hotel room in the city center of Liverpool. Our flight out of Raleigh, North Carolina, was fine. We had to change at JFK, and it was there that we noticed several people wearing face masks.

We picked up the rental car and drove straight to the hotel in Liverpool to drop off our suitcases. I made the first visit to my mum and dad alone, knowing it would be very overwhelming and emotional. A few days passed, and we spent as much time as we could with my dad, allowing Alison time to get to know him.

We found ourselves in our hotel room at 10:00 p.m. one night. I was unable to sleep. Alison and I sat up talking and crying. Around 2:00 a.m., I heard music outside the hotel window. I should mention, we were on the 4th floor, right in the city center of Liverpool. Our hotel window faced over the busy streets filled with shops, restaurants, bars, and nightclubs.

This music wasn't coming from a bar or nightclub; it was coming from a busker. We sat on the windowsill of our hotel room and looked down at a man playing his guitar, singing "Sweet Caroline" by Neil Diamond. For some unknown reason, I broke down and couldn't stop crying. Alison held me tight. My dad was dying, and there was nothing I could do.

Our week was up, so we said our goodbyes before leaving for the airport. Little did I know that the pandemic would cause a travel ban, and I wouldn't see my dad again until November 2020, just two days before he passed.

Since that night in Liverpool, hearing "Sweet Caroline" reminds me of my dad. Fast forward three years to March 2023, it was like any other normal day. Alison had been to the office, returned home, we had dinner, and later, we went to bed. I put my cell phone on its charger on my nightstand and fell asleep. At 1:16 a.m., I woke up.

What woke me? My cell phone was playing "Sweet Caroline" loudly! I reached over and grabbed my phone. The screen lit up and showed the home page. There were no apps open, but the song was playing as clear as day! Pandora was not open, and I don't have that song saved to my phone, so how could it be playing?

I tried to stop the song from playing. I pressed all the buttons, yet it continued. Finally, I shut the phone off. I looked around the dark bedroom and called out to my dad, "Dad, are you there? Is that you?"

Alison, startled awake by the song, was also in shock. We were both shaking. We knew what that song meant to us, but we had no idea how it began to play on my phone. I have no doubt that it was my dad.

The following week I was a guest speaker on a podcast in Australia. I shared this story with the host, Ian, and his listeners. Ian then pointed out that I should look in the Bible, at Romans 1:16.

It was 1.16 a.m. when the song played. Romans 1:16 reads, "For I am not ashamed of the gospel, because it is the power of God that brings salvation to everyone who believes: first to the Jew, then to the Gentile" (*New International Version Bible*, 2011/1978, Romans 1:16). To me, that tells me that my dad is alive. "The power of God that brings salvation to everyone who believes." Isn't that saying that if we believe we will find salvation? My dad believed it.

A Moment of Reflection

It's remarkable to reflect on the diverse perspectives we've encountered along this path. From the deeply spiritual insights of various religions to the philosophical musings of theologians, the evocative imagery of poets and artists, and the analytical scrutiny of scientists, each realm offers its own unique lens through which we can contemplate the great beyond.

Religion brings comfort to people during difficult times through its beliefs and rituals. Whether it's the hope of seeing loved ones in the afterlife, the idea of karma and rebirth, or the concept of spiritual growth, faith helps us make sense of life and death. The study of theology further examines these beliefs, pondering issues like divine fairness, destiny, and the essence of the soul—encouraging us to reflect on our spiritual beliefs.

Poetry, with its power to evoke emotion and transcend language, paints vivid portraits of Heaven's beauty and mystery. Through the words of poets, we see glimpses of an ethereal realm where time stands still and love knows no bounds. Science, meanwhile, approaches the afterlife with a lens of inquiry, probing the mysteries of consciousness, near-death experiences, and the nature of reality itself. While science may not offer definitive answers to the questions of what lies beyond, it invites us to marvel at the wonder of existence and the vastness of the cosmos.

But, perhaps, the true beauty lies in the diversity of these perspectives. In a world where grief touches us all in different ways, having a multitude of interpretations of Heaven and the afterlife allows each of us to find our own path to healing and understanding. What resonates deeply with one person may not hold the same significance for another, and that's perfectly okay. In this wide array of beliefs and ideas, we are free to explore, question, and seek out the answers that speak to our hearts.

As we conclude our exploration, let's appreciate the beauty of variety. Let's take comfort in knowing that, despite differences, there's space for everyone to discover their truth.

The Healing Path Through Grief

If you chose this book, there is a good chance you've known the ache of loss. Maybe you've lost a loved one, a friend, a pet, or even a piece of yourself along the way. Grief is a path we all must walk at some point in our lives, and while it may seem like an endless battle of pain, I want you to know that there's healing and comfort waiting for you. The first step is to understand that you get to write the timeline. There is no rush; there is no deadline.

Acknowledging your grief, truly feeling the depths of your emotions, is important while healing. It's not easy, I know. In fact, it may feel like you're drowning. But, acknowledging your grief is like unlocking a door to a hidden chamber within yourself. It's a sacred space where you can honor your feelings, your memories, and your loved ones.

Here's why acknowledging your grief is so important:

- **Emotional release:** Allowing yourself to feel your emotions gives you an outlet to release pent-up feelings of sadness, anger, guilt, or regret. Bottling up emotions only prolongs the healing process.

- **Connection:** Sharing your grief with others fosters connection and support. You'll find comfort in knowing that you're not alone in your pain, and you may even discover new depths of empathy and compassion within yourself.

- **Honoring memories:** By acknowledging your grief, you pay tribute to the memories of your loved ones. You keep their spirit alive in your heart, cherishing the moments you shared together and finding comfort in the legacy they've left behind.

- **Healing:** Grief is a natural response to loss, and allowing yourself to grieve is essential for healing. It's through the process of recognizing, feeling, and expressing your grief that you'll find the strength to live on with hope and resilience.

Now, I understand that the path of grief is different for everyone. But here are some suggestions to help you grieve in a healthy manner:

- **Create rituals**: Establishing rituals or traditions in honor of your loved one can serve as comforting anchors in the tumultuous sea of grief. These rituals don't need to be elaborate; even simple acts like lighting a candle at a certain time each day, visiting a place that holds special memories, or writing letters to your loved one can provide solace and a sense of connection. Rituals offer a tangible way to express your love and keep the memory of your loved one alive.

- **Ask for help**: Grieving is a deeply personal experience, but it doesn't have to be a solitary journey. Reach out to friends, family, or a support group who can offer understanding and validation during this challenging time. Surrounding yourself with compassionate individuals who listen without judgment can provide invaluable support. Don't hesitate to ask for help when you need it; allowing others to share in your grief can lighten the burden and foster healing.

- **Express yourself**: Grief can evoke a whirlwind of emotions, from sadness and anger to love and gratitude. Finding healthy outlets to express these feelings is essential for your emotional well-being. Whether it's through writing in a journal, creating art, playing music, or engaging in physical activity, find what resonates with you and allows you to release pent-up emotions. Expressing yourself in constructive ways can be cathartic and help you navigate the complexities of grief with greater ease.

- **Practice self-compassion**: Within the pain of loss, it's crucial to extend kindness and compassion to yourself. Give yourself permission to grieve in your own way and at your own pace. Allow yourself moments of rest and reflection, prioritize self-care activities that nourish your body and soul, and engage in activities that bring you comfort and joy. Remember, grieving is a natural and necessary process, and it's okay to take the time you need to heal.

- **Seek professional help**: If you find yourself struggling to cope with your grief or experiencing overwhelming emotions that interfere with daily life, don't hesitate to seek the guidance of a therapist or counselor. These trained professionals can offer a safe and supportive space for you to explore your feelings, provide coping strategies tailored to your individual needs, and support you on your journey toward healing. Seeking professional help is a courageous step toward self-care and can empower you to navigate the challenges of grief with resilience and strength.

For those who have lost loved ones and continue to struggle, it can often be associated with that feeling of them being *gone*. Honoring our loved ones who have passed away is a beautiful way to keep their memory alive and celebrate the impact they've had on our lives. It helps fill that void. Here are some heartfelt ways to honor them:

- **Create a memory book:** Compile photos, letters, and mementos that remind you of your loved one into a scrapbook or memory book. This tangible keepsake can serve as a cherished reminder of the special moments you shared together.

- **Plant a memorial garden:** Dedicate a garden or plant a tree in memory of your loved one. Watching flowers bloom or a tree grow can be a comforting and symbolic way to honor their life and legacy.

- **Donate to a cause:** Consider donating to a charitable organization or cause that was meaningful to your loved one. Whether it's a scholarship fund, animal shelter, or medical research foundation, giving back in their name can be a powerful way to honor their memory and continue their legacy of kindness and generosity.

- **Hold a memorial service:** Organize a memorial service or gathering to celebrate the life of your loved one with friends and family. Share stories, anecdotes, and memories, and take comfort in the love and support of those who knew and cared for them.

- **Create a tribute video:** Compile photos, videos, and music to create a tribute video honoring your loved one's life and accomplishments. Share it with friends and family, or keep it as a personal keepsake to revisit whenever you need a reminder of their presence.

- **Perform acts of kindness:** Pay tribute to your loved one by performing acts of kindness in their memory. Whether it's volunteering at a local shelter, helping a neighbor in need, or simply spreading love and positivity, these acts honor their spirit and continue the ripple effect of their love and compassion in the world.

- **Celebrate special days:** Honor your loved one on special occasions such as birthdays, anniversaries, or holidays by participating in activities they enjoyed or sharing a meal in their memory. Raise a toast, make their favorite meal for dinner, or say a prayer to honor their presence and the love you still carry in your heart.

- **Keep their traditions alive:** Continue traditions or rituals that were important to your loved one. Whether it's playing their favorite song or participating in a cherished family holiday tradition, keeping these practices alive can provide comfort and connection to their memory.

- **Create a memorial fund:** Establish a memorial fund or scholarship in your loved one's name to support causes or initiatives that were important to them. This lasting tribute ensures that their memory lives on and makes a positive impact in the lives of others for years to come.

- **Live their values:** Honor your loved one by embodying the values and principles they lived by. Whether it's kindness, compassion, resilience, or courage, strive to carry their legacy forward by living a life that reflects the love and wisdom they imparted to you.

In honoring our loved ones, we not only keep their memory alive but, also, find comfort in the everlasting bond we shared with them.

Remember, grief is not a sign of weakness; it's a testament to the depth of your love. So embrace your grief, honor your emotions, and trust that—in time—the pain will soften and the memories will bring you peace.

As we finish this chapter, I hope you feel a warm comfort in your heart, hope in your spirit, and a renewed sense of wonder about the mysteries beyond our earthly life.

We've thought about a heavenly place where souls are happy forever with a loving Creator. We've also explored the idea of souls being reborn in different lives to learn and grow. Lastly, we've pondered on the concept of all souls coming together as one cosmic entity beyond time and space.

Within all the different viewpoints, one truth stands out: Love lasts forever, connecting us all and offering guidance, comfort, and unity.

As we go through the difficult emotions of grief and loss, let's remember that love is limitless and goes beyond death. Even though our loved ones may pass away, their love stays with us like a gentle breeze or a sweet melody in our hearts.

In our sadness, let's find comfort in treasured memories, shared moments, and love. Let's honor those who passed by living purposefully, kindly, and compassionately—believing they watch over us.

CONCLUSION

... ◈ ...

I feel blessed to be sitting here, reflecting on the journey we've taken together through the mysteries of Heaven. I'm struck by the depth of the human spirit and its relentless quest for understanding. The genesis of this odyssey lies in the profound loss I experienced when my father succumbed to cancer in 2020. Raised within the folds of Catholicism, his passing stirred within me a whirlwind of questions that begged to be explored.

There were questions about existence, the nature of the soul, and what lies beyond the threshold of mortal life. And so, fueled by grief and an insatiable curiosity, I started on a writing journey that led me to this moment, penning my fifth book, dedicated entirely to unraveling the enigma of Heaven.

This voyage has been one of discovery, guided by the flickering flames of faith, reason, and introspection. We've moved through the rich and diverse belief systems, pausing to listen to the whispers of Muslims. We visited what their beliefs are about Heaven. We uncovered that in Islam, Heaven is often referred to as *Jannah*, which translates to "Paradise" in English. It is depicted as a place of eternal bliss and reward for those who have lived righteous lives according to the teachings of Islam.

We then visited the world of Judaism. We discovered that in Judaism, the concept of an afterlife, including the belief in Heaven, varies among different denominations and interpretations. In the Hebrew Bible (the *Tanakh*), there are limited references to an afterlife, and the focus tends to be more on the earthly realm and fulfilling one's responsibilities to God and society during one's lifetime.

We also explored Buddhism. We uncovered that In Buddhism, the concept of Heaven is often interpreted within the framework of the cycle of birth, death, and rebirth—known as *samsara*. While Buddhism does acknowledge various heavenly realms or celestial abodes, they are not considered eternal or permanent states like the concept of Heaven in some other religions.

We spent time outside of the religious sectors and wandered through the hallowed halls of theology, pondering the musings of scholars and mystics alike, each offering a fragment of truth to add to our collective understanding.

But our exploration did not stop there. No, we ventured further into the realm where science meets spirituality, where the empirical and the ethereal converge. In our quest for truth, we've grappled with the paradoxes and mysteries that shroud the concept of Heaven, acknowledging that while science may offer explanations grounded in observable phenomena, it is often our faith that provides the anchor in times of uncertainty.

Within the many different beliefs and ideas, one clear truth stands out: the power of belief. Whether Heaven is seen as a beautiful place, a state of higher awareness, or a symbol of eternal peace, our belief in it gives us hope in tough times. It's like a guiding light in the darkness, helping us through sadness by showing us that love is limitless and the connections we make in life are unbreakable even in death.

As we bid farewell, I implore you to carry with you the lessons and revelations that have unfolded within these pages. Let them serve as a compass on your journey through grief and healing, illuminating the path ahead with the gentle glow of understanding and acceptance.

And if, in the quiet moments of reflection, you find comfort in the words shared here—I ask for your support. Leave a review, share your thoughts, and help extend the reach of this book to those who may find themselves on a healing path of grief.

In parting, remember this: Though the road may be long and the burdens heavy, you are not alone. You are loved, and you carry within you the light of hope that can never be extinguished.

Be blessed and may your God go with you.

John

REFERENCES

Allen, J. (2022a). *Keep calm and cope with grief: 9 chapters for managing fear and grief when losing a parent or loved one.* Independently published.

Allen, J. (2022b). *Life after this: 9 chapters: History shows we have contacted the deceased and you can do it, too.* Independently published.

Allen, J. (2022c). *Nature's reach: Coping with grief the natural way.* Independently published.

Andrade, G. (n.d.). Immortality. *Internet Encyclopedia of Philosophy.* https://iep.utm.edu/immortal/

Atsma, A. (n.d.). *Elysium—Islands of the blessed of Greek mythology.* Theoi Project. https://www.theoi.com/Kosmos/Elysion.html

Ayoub, O. (2021a, July 31). Life after death in Islam: The concept and the 14 stages of afterlife. *Zamzam Blogs.* https://zamzam.com/blog/life-after-death-in-islam/

Ayoub, O. (2021b, July 31). 7 levels of heaven in Islam, surahs of Jannah in the Quran. *Zamzam Blogs.* https://zamzam.com/blog/seven-levels-of-heaven/

Barr, S. M. (2022, April 5). *Is science of any help in thinking about Heaven?* Church Life Journal. https://churchlifejournal.nd.edu/articles/is-science-of-any-help-in-thinking-about-heaven/

Belief in judgement day. (2014, August 13). Why Islam. https://www.whyislam.org/belief-in-judgement-day/

The Bible: English Standard Version. (2016). Bible Gateway. https://www.biblegateway.com/ (Original work published 2001)

Bonding with your baby. (n.d.). Nemours Kids Health. https://kidshealth.org/en/parents/bonding.html

Buddhist cosmology. (n.d.). *Freeing oneself from suffering and its causes.* https://buddhist-spirituality.com/other-buddhism-topics/buddhist-cosmology

Carr, D., & Sharp, S. (2014). Do afterlife beliefs affect psychological adjustment to late-life spousal loss? *The Journals of Gerontology Series B, 69B*(1), 103–112. https://doi.org/10.1093/geronb/gbt063

CBS News. (2014, February 25). *Study: People who believe in Heaven happier with their lives.* https://www.cbsnews.com/news/people-who-believe-in-heaven-happier-with-their-lives-according-to-study/

Childs-Heyl, J. (2023, March 22). *Inner child work: How your past shapes your present.* Verywell Mind. https://www.verywellmind.com/inner-child-work-how-your-past-shapes-your-present-7152929

Christian Pure Team. (2023, December 25). *Will we remember our loved ones in Heaven?* Christian Pure. https://www.christianpure.com/blog/remember-loved-ones-in-heaven

Critchley, P. (n.d.). The visionary materialism of William Blake. *Academia.* https://www.academia.edu/6582196/The_Visionary_Materialism_of_William_Blake

Do the souls meet in al-Barzakh? (2009, January 21). Islam Question & Answer. https://islamqa.info/en/answers/20820/do-the-souls-meet-in-al-barzakh

Edmonds, R. G., III. (2014). A lively afterlife and beyond: The soul in Plato, Homer, and the Orphica. *Études Platoniciennes, 11.* https://doi.org/10.4000/etudesplatoniciennes.517

English Standard Version. (2016). 1 Corinthians 15 ESV. Biblehub.com. https://biblehub.com/esv/1_corinthians/15.htm

Fitouchi, L., & Singh, M. (2022). Supernatural punishment beliefs as cognitively compelling tools of social control. *Current Opinion in Psychology, 44,* 252–257. https://doi.org/10.1016/j.copsyc.2021.09.022

Flowers, B. (n.d.). *Grief and spirituality: A journey towards comfort.* Farewelling. https://www.myfarewelling.com/article/grief-and-spirituality-a-journey-towards-comfort

Glenn, C. (2015, April 10). Abandon hope: Dante, Swedenborg, and the eternity of Hell. *Good and Truth.* https://www.patheos.com/blogs/goodandtruth/2015/04/abandon-hope-dante-swedenborg-and-the-eternity-of-hell/

The Holy Bible: King James Version. (2011). Hendrickson. (Original work published 1611)

Holy Bible, New Living Translation. (2015). BibleGateway. https://www.biblegateway.com/versions/New-Living-Translation-NLT-Bible/ (Original work published 1996)

Isaiah 66:1. (n.d.). Bible Study Tools. https://www.biblestudytools.com/commentaries/gills-exposition-of-the-bible/isaiah-66-1.html

Johnson, S. (2021, August 6). What does Jainism teach about death & the afterlife? *Join Cake.* https://www.joincake.com/blog/jainism-afterlife/

Journey to the afterlife. (n.d.). The British Museum. https://www.britishmuseum.org/learn/schools/ages-7-11/ancient-egypt/journey-afterlife

Kara-Ivanov Kaniel, R. (2019, September 20). *Feminine aspects of repentance*. Jewish Independent. https://www.jewishindependent.ca/feminine-aspects-of-repentance/

King James Bible. (2017). 2 Corinthians 12:2-4. Bible Hub. https://biblehub.com/kjv/2_corinthians/12.htm (Original work published 1769)

Koch, C. (2020, June 1). What near-death experiences reveal about the brain. *Scientific American*. https://www.scientificamerican.com/article/what-near-death-experiences-reveal-about-the-brain/

Kramer, S. N. (1964, May). The Indus civilization and Dilmun, the Sumerian paradise land. *Expedition Magazine, 6*(3), 44–52. https://www.penn.museum/sites/expedition/the-indus-civilization-and-dilmun-the-sumerian-paradise-land/

Lichfield, G. (2015, April). The science of near-death experiences. *The Atlantic*. https://www.theatlantic.com/magazine/archive/2015/04/the-science-of-near-death-experiences/386231/

Line upon line: Romans 1:16. (n.d.). Churchofjesuschrist.org. https://www.churchofjesuschrist.org/study/new-era/2012/09/share-the-gospel/line-upon-line-romans-1-16?lang=eng

Long, J. (2014). Near-Death experiences evidence for their reality. *Missouri Medicine, 111*(5), 372–380. https://www.ncbi.nlm.nih.gov/pmc/articles/PMC6172100/

Magis Center. (2024, January 24). 5 credible stories of near death experiences. *Magis Center*. https://www.magiscenter.com/blog/credible-near-death-experience-stories

Marks, K. (2024, February 6). *18 of the greatest religious leaders in history*. Owlcation. https://owlcation.com/humanities/10-Greatest-Religious-Leaders-in-History

McDannell, C., & Lang, B. (1988). *Heaven: A history*. Yale University Press. https://www.jstor.org/stable/j.ctt1cc2k45

New American Standard Bible. (1995). Isaiah 13:10. Biblia. https://biblia.com/bible/nasb95/isaiah/13/10 (Original work published 1971)

New International Version Bible. (2011). The NIV Bible. https://www.thenivbible.com (Original work published 1978)

The New King James Version. (1982). Luke 16:19–31. Biblia. https://biblia.com/bible/nkjv/luke/16/19-31

Noonan, J. (2023, May 1). *What happens to your soul when you die? The afterlife revealed*. Finding Dulcinea. https://www.findingdulcinea.com/what-happens-to-your-soul-when-you-die/

Oberhaus, D. (2017, July 27). *Near-Death experiences have a freakish amount in common*. Vice. https://www.vice.com/en/article/vbmw89/near-death-experiences-have-a-freakish-amount-in-common

Pew Research Center. (2021, November 23). *Few Americans blame God or say faith has been shaken amid pandemic, other tragedies*. https://www.pewresearch.org/religion/2021/11/23/few-americans-blame-god-or-say-faith-has-been-shaken-amid-pandemic-other-tragedies/

The Qur'an (M.A.S Abdel Haleem, Trans.). (2004). Oxford University Press.

Rich, T. R. (n.d.). *Olam Ha-Ba: The afterlife*. Judaism 101; Jew FAQ. https://www.jewfaq.org/afterlife

Rowlandson, W. (2011). Borges's reading of Dante and Swedenborg: Mysticism and the real. *Variaciones Borges, 32*, 59–85. https://www.jstor.org/stable/24881527

Saint Thomas Aquinas. (2023, August 9). Biography. https://www.biography.com/religious-figure/saint-thomas-aquinas

Sayler, G. (2007, March 23). Heaven and Hell, according to various religions. *Neatorama.* https://www.neatorama.com/2007/03/23/heaven-and-hell-according-to-various-religions/

Shariff, A. F., & Aknin, L. B. (2014). The emotional toll of Hell: Cross-National and experimental evidence for the negative well-being effects of Hell beliefs. *PLoS ONE, 9*(1), e85251. https://doi.org/10.1371/journal.pone.0085251

Sheng Yen, C. M. (2007). *Orthodox Chinese Buddhism* (D. Gildow, Trans.; pp. 31–41). Dharma Drum Publication. http://www.108wisdom.org/html/OTH_03.pdf

Smethurst, M. (n.d.). *Is there proof of Heaven?* Explore God. https://www.exploregod.com/articles/is-there-proof-of-heaven

Travers, M. (2022, July 10). Psychological consequences of believing in Heaven and Hell. *Psychology Today.* https://www.psychologytoday.com/us/blog/social-instincts/202207/psychological-consequences-believing-in-heaven-and-hell

Via. (2022, July 15). *The cave and the light | Reflections & notes.* Vialogue. https://vialogue.wordpress.com/2022/07/15/the-cave-and-the-light-reflections-notes/

Waddle, J. (2023, December 20). *10 beautiful* biblical *descriptions of what Heaven will look like and be like.* Crosswalk.com. https://www.crosswalk.com/faith/bible-study/10-beautiful-descriptions-of-heaven-from-the-bible.html

Weber, J. (2021, November 23). *Heaven and Hell: Americans answer 20 questions on who goes and what happens.* Christianity Today. https://www.christianitytoday.com/news/2021/november/heaven-hell-universalism-reincarnation-pew-afterlife-survey.html

What does Isaiah 13:10 mean? (n.d.). BibleRef.com. https://www.bibleref.com/Isaiah/13/Isaiah-13-10.html

What does Isaiah 66:1 mean? (n.d.). BibleRef.com. https://www.bibleref.com/Isaiah/66/Isaiah-66-1.html

What does Matthew 19:16 mean? (n.d.). BibleRef.com. https://www.bibleref.com/Matthew/19/Matthew-19-16.html

What does Psalm 8:3 mean? (n.d.). BibleRef.com. https://www.bibleref.com/Psalms/8/Psalm-8-3.html

What does Psalm 104:12 mean? (n.d.). BibleRef.com. https://www.bibleref.com/Psalms/104/Psalm-104-12.html

What does 2 Corinthians 12:2 mean? (n.d.). BibleRef.com. https://www.bibleref.com/2-Corinthians/12/2-Corinthians-12-2.html

Why is being a good person not enough to get you into Heaven? (2022, January 4). GotQuestions.org. https://www.gotquestions.org/good-person.html

Image References

aitoff. (2016, February 18). *Loving, memory, memorial* [Image]. Pixabay. https://pixabay.com/photos/loving-memory-memorial-grief-1207568/

beingboring. (2019, August 14). *Mosque-Abu Dhabi* [Image]. Pixabay. https://pixabay.com/photos/mosque-abu-dhabi-u-a-e-architecture-4403790/

BlenderTimer. (2019, August 26). *Chipmunk, mammal, animal* [Image]. Pixabay. https://pixabay.com/photos/chipmunk-mammal-animal-rodent-4432117/

dgenge. (2021, July 19). *Dachsund dog angel tattoo* [Image]. Pixabay. https://pixabay.com/vectors/dog-heaven-pet-angel-animal-6471637/

EddieKphoto. (2021, September 25). *Couple, elderly, walking* [Image]. Pixabay. https://pixabay.com/photos/couple-elderly-walking-fall-trail-6653517/

geralt. (2019, January 8). *Light tunnel silhouette* [Image]. Pixabay. https://pixabay.com/illustrations/light-tunnel-silhouette-woman-3920898/

geralt. (2015, June 14). *Clouds Heaven faith* [Image]. Pixabay. https://pixabay.com/illustrations/clouds-heaven-faith-christianity-806637/

Johnhain. (2017, May 1). *Sitting meditate being* [Image]. Pixabay. https://pixabay.com/illustrations/sitting-meditate-being-here-now-2267581/

KELLEPICS. (2017, October 16). *Fantasy, light, mood* [Image]. Pixabay. https://pixabay.com/photos/fantasy-light-mood-heaven-lovely-2861107/

LaurBadea. (2016, December 19). *Mountain, sunset, Heaven* [Image]. Pixabay. https://pixabay.com/photos/mountain-sunset-heaven-silhouette-1919186/

mantab. (2018, September 14). *Heaven, the way, angel* [Image]. Pixabay. https://pixabay.com/photos/heaven-the-way-angel-salvation-3676393/

Myriams-Fotos. (2016, February 24). *Pray, rosary, faith* [Image]. Pixabay. https://pixabay.com/photos/pray-rosary-faith-religion-1218506/

12019. (2016, October 22). *Autumn, street, leaves* [Image]. Pixabay. https://pixabay.com/photos/autumn-street-leaves-lane-foliage-1758194/

photosforyou. (2014, January 6). *Buddha, statue, Hong Kong* [Image]. Pixabay. https://pixabay.com/photos/buddha-statue-hong-kong-asian-240211/

sciencefreak. (2014, December 27). *Angel wing feathers* [Image]. Pixabay. https://pixabay.com/illustrations/angel-wing-feathers-heavenly-god-574647/

7753727. (2018, January 20). *Sculpture, statue, Cordoba* [Image]. Pixabay. https://pixabay.com/photos/sculpture-statue-cordoba-andalusia-3092121/

Wal_172619. (2020, March 25). *Read scripture book* [Image]. Pixabay. https://pixabay.com/photos/read-scripture-book-holy-book-4960517/

Yuri_B. (2019, March 14). *Angel, grim, moon* [Image]. Pixabay. https://pixabay.com/photos/angel-grim-moon-background-fantasy-4057032/

Made in the USA
Middletown, DE
26 August 2024

59808194R00092